Contents

University of Plymouth Library

Subject to status this item may be renewed
via your Voyager account

http://voyager.plymouth.ac.uk

Exeter tel: (01392) 475049
Exmouth tel: (01395) 255331
Plymouth tel: (01752) 232323

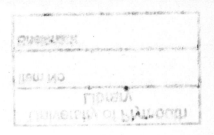

Blaming Ourselves: September 11 and the Agony of the Left

**Edited by Gregory Melleuish
and Imre Salusinszky**

Foreword by Barry Cohen

Duffy & Snellgrove
Sydney

Published by Duffy & Snellgrove in 2002
PO Box 177 Potts Point NSW 1335 Australia
info@duffyandsnellgrove.com.au

Earlier versions of the essays by Owen Harries and
Keith Windschuttle have appeared in
The National Interest and *Quadrant*, respectively.

Distributed by Pan Macmillan

Cover design by Alex Snellgrove
Typeset by Cooper Graphics
Printed by Griffin Press

ISBN 1 876631 37 6

visit our website: www.duffyandsnellgrove.com.au

Foreword

Barry Cohen

I imagine my emotions were no different to most people's. Disbelief preceded shock before turning to seething rage. The nausea commenced when I started reading the anti-American tirade in the columns and letters to the editor section of the *Sydney Morning Herald*. How much the world changed on September 11 is yet to be determined but for me it ended some long friendships. There are many quoted in this book whom I have no wish to speak to again.

Have only one problem with the book and that is in the title, *Blaming Ourselves: September 11 and the Agony of the Left*. Having always regarded myself as being 'of the Left', I resent being lumped in with those who wrote such vile rubbish. Fortunately the editors drew a distinction between the intellectual left and mainstream Labor who, they correctly pointed out, 'acted throughout the crisis with great honour and sound judgement'.

What they failed to mention was the influence the intellectual left will have on Labor policy through the media, academe and Party forums. Pouring scorn on all those who support the war on terrorism will be their method of silencing them. Branding them 'hardline right-wingers' will help erode support in pre-selections and caucus ballots. Only the courageous and foolhardy will speak up. It would have been difficult to support the United States with Clinton in the White House. It will be dubya hard with his successor.

If there is a surprise in this book it is that so many of the essayists seemed surprised by the lunacy of the Left. It was ever thus. Stalin, Mao, Castro, Pol Pot, Saddam et al were never short of admirers from that quarter. Even when their monstrous crimes were revealed the Left never showed the slightest sign of contrition. One of the nice things about being a member of the Left is never having to admit you're wrong. When the Cold War ended they didn't miss a beat as they moved on to a range of other worthy causes that provided platforms for them to express their hatred of all things capitalist and American.

If nothing else September 11 revealed how much the quality media had deteriorated in recent years. World-wide it quickly became evident that while television provided excellent coverage of what actually happened there was a noticeable shortage of specialist journalists to explain why it happened.

When the bean-counters took control of media empires and decided that what interested the masses was life-style issues rather than politics and foreign affairs the media concentrated on fashion, food, wine, housing, décor and other such matters of great moment. What passes for current affairs on television is now mindless trivia.

Foreign affairs journalists, who had specialist knowledge of particular regions, were replaced in the opinion pages by a motley collection of academics, public institute operatives, politicians, and syndicated columnists primarily because they can get them for next to nothing. Gone were the days when the *Sydney Morning Herald*, the *Australian* and *The Age* had foreign affairs specialists. Suddenly journalists who had spent years in the Canberra press gallery were expected to write knowingly about international affairs. Most were not up to it.

Short of local specialists the same papers drew on such unbiased sources as *The Observer*, *The Guardian* and Arab academics. All were able to agree that America was being run by a pack of fools. Most of our local scribes followed the anti-American line pushed so aciduously by the Left.

That the Americans brought the massacre on themselves due to their flawed foreign policy was restated endlessly as if it was a self-evident truth. No detailed analysis was provided with the only specific example being America's failure to 'rein in' the Israelis. Such silly generalisations were insulting to anyone with an IQ above room temperature. All the ills that beset the Islamic world were clearly Israel's – the Soviet Union's invasion of Afghanistan, the Iraq/Iran war, Saddam's invasion of Kuwait, the Balkan conflict and the bloody internal clashes in the Sudan, Algeria, Syria and Iraq. IT was amazing that so many Australian journalists swallowed and then regurgitated such guff. However when one considers how few have any knowledge of the Middle East it was not all that surprising. Peering down from the Canberra press gallery may make you an expert on Australian politics but it does little to equip you to comment on what is happening in the Middle East.

Blaming Ourselves is a book that needed to be written.

It was long overdue for conservatives and genuine liberals to take on the intellectual thugs of the 'progressive' Left and to stop feeling guilty about supporting the United States. Never has the line between good and evil been so clearly drawn.

For too long the Left have been able to enjoy the affluence created by American capitalism and take shelter behind the American defense umbrella while at the same time reserving the right to pour out their hatred of all things American. They take the best the Americans have to offer then spit in their face.

Unlike Australians, Americans aren't perfect. They've made mistakes but they are a decent people who believe passionately in the things the majority of Australians hold dear – freedom and democracy. Thank God that when the Cold War ended it was America who was left standing. Imagine for one minute the awful alternative.

Not since the end of World War II has it been more important for Americans to know that the hatred that permeated the columns and the letter to the editor pages of the Australian press do not represent the views of the majority of Australians. The book will kick-start that process.

The Honourable Barry Cohen *was Minister for Arts, Heritage and the Environment, 1983-1987. He now runs the Calga Springs Wildlife Sanctuary on the NSW Central Coast, with his son, Adam.*

Introduction

Gregory Melleuish and Imre Salusinszky

The horrific events of September 11 have left an indelible mark on the world and become a defining moment in the history of the twenty-first century. They demonstrate that the hard won victories of the twentieth century over brutality, fanaticism and totalitarianism did not spell the 'end of history'. Such evils are always with us.

There was, however, a double shock associated with September 11: the viciousness of the events themselves and the callousness of many of the responses to the events, particularly by those who call themselves left 'humanitarians', as they sought to blame the victim and so excuse the transgressor. This was truly shocking, as this had been an attack on civilisation and the virtues that a civilised existence embodies – openness, civility and tolerance – in the name of a narrow-minded fanaticism that demonises those who do not share its vision of the world. Such a state of affairs cries out to be understood.

One of the reasons why the events of September 11 and their aftermath can be called a 'defining moment' is because of their impact on the lives of large numbers of people. At one level this impact can be seen in terms of psychological stress, nightmares and general trauma. At another level it is a defining moment because it has elicited a whole range of thoughtful and reflective responses on matters of universal importance, such as the nature of civilisation and civilised life, and the meaning of a free society. These essays deal with these sorts of concerns. In so doing they do not seek to propagate a party line beyond a basic agreement that a free liberal society is the most desirable form of polity. In coming to terms with September 11 these essays have focused around a number of themes, in particular the role of intellectuals, the nature of Western civilisation, and the character of a liberal polity.

As this volume demonstrates there are a variety of views regarding both what Western civilisation is and what ails it. For most liberals the Enlightenment is the key defining moment in the coming of modernity but there is some disagreement regarding the split amongst modern intellectuals that followed from it. For some, following David Gress, the key division is between what he calls the sceptical and radical Enlightenments; for others, the key lies in the opposition between the Enlightenment and Romanticism. But the differences perhaps may be more apparent than real: is Rousseau, for example, to be considered a member of the radical Enlightenment or a key figure in the Romantic movement?

In either case there can be no doubt regarding the unique turn that modern Western civilisation took as it broke out of the agrarian mould of all previous civilisations. Moreover, as both John Pocock and Pierre Manent have argued, the Enlightenment saw the creation of a new ethos for this new type of civilisation that brought together civility, tolerance and 'sweet commerce'. This ethos replaced older ideals based on the warrior and on the religious life.

This new civilisation generated a lot of enemies, both internal and external. The internal enemies were intellectuals who were shocked by the nature of the new order, and who simultaneously poured scorn on its failings while dreaming of utopias to replace it. The Enlightenment spawned 'grub street', full of creatures such as Marat, who specialised in defamation, vilification and pornography and, when the opportunity beckoned, violent revolution. This was but the taste of things to come.

Externally other mighty civilisations, which were civilised when Europe was run by a bunch of smelly, illiterate oafs, were mightily put out by the surge of Western civilisation, in particular China and the Islamic world. Islam has had a long, complex and often difficult relationship with the West because it can also claim the heritage of Athens and Jerusalem. In fact Islam traditionally could consider itself to be a superior embodiment of that heritage.

Many intellectuals of both the Western and the non-Western world are offended by modern civilisation because it wounds their self-esteem and pride. What is best termed a clerisy, institutional intellectuals dependent on the public purse, was an important element of agrarian civilisation when literacy was not widespread, but it has lost much of its status in the contemporary world. The new intellectuals of the Enlightenment who advocated the cause of civility and commerce were not members of a clerisy, and interestingly this is largely true of the contributors to this volume. The clerisy finds only modest compensation in the many material benefits provided by modern civilisation. They find it vulgar and ostentatious because they tend to consider themselves to be true aristocrats in a world full of low or popular culture, or what is usually called democracy.

For many intellectuals over the past two hundred years, the hatred for commerce and the bourgeoisie has become so overwhelming that they have sought simultaneously to destroy it totally and to create some sort of ideal world. This has been true of anarchists, Nazis, communists, terrorists and latterly Islamist extremists. The enemies of modern civilisation have always fallen into two classes. First, there has been an extremely small minority willing to put their lives on the line, driven by total hatred and rejection of what they see as corruption, evil and decadence. In their own eyes they are highly moral people, not doing it for personal gain or for any materialist motive, but simply motivated by the desire to restore the world to moral purity. Then there are those who are 'fellow travellers' and gain a vicarious satisfaction from contemplating the actions of the extremists. They fantasise about punishing modern civilisation but enjoy too much the lifestyle it provides to engage in any action.

In the face of such enemies there is a continuing need to state the case for civilisation, to re-assert the importance of civilised values and point to the absurdity of trying to create goodness through acts of extraordinary evil. This is a major goal of this collection.

But many of the pieces in this book also have a more critical, or negative, ambition: to provide a permanent memorial to the intemperance of the intellectual left. In the days and weeks following September 11, ordinary Australians felt neither a clash of their loyalties, nor a division of their sympathies: they were simply revolted by what had been perpetrated against the United States, and felt an immediate and unmediated wave of identification with their American cousins. And it did not seem to them grotesque, or even passingly anomalous, that their feelings were much more intense than in the case of numerically equivalent disasters involving people with whom they did not share the same rich and complex skein of personal, cultural, and linguistic connections.

For the intellectuals of the left, however, it was all just … too much. The situation, as we kept hearing, was more ideologically 'complex' than we were being led to believe (complexity in such situations being, as the critic John Gross has remarked, the last refuge of the scoundrel).

Where was all the complexity? Why would we even think of blaming anyone but the terrorists, and those who support them? Well, in the first place, the conflict on and since September 11 is a conflict between freedom and fascism, always a teaser for the intellectuals, whose tradition of hatred for economic and individual freedom – for the open society – has many points in common with fascism. Even more tricky, from this angle, was the fact that some of the rhetoric used by that noted anti-globalisation activist, Osama bin Laden, clearly derived from the same European anti-capitalist sources – Fanon, Sorel, Sartre, and others – that had nourished the New Left in the 1970s.

And how galling that so many of the objects of the unprecedented wave of international sympathy following September 11 were members of the very professional group – finance-sector workers – whom *Sydney*

Morning Herald television critic Doug Anderson had once memorably described as 'parasite scum' (adding the explanatory note that 'any excuse for venality is acceptable in the business world').

Second, we cannot forget that the attack that took place on the 11th was upon the intellectuals' most treasured hate-object, the Great Satan himself. Incinerating the World Trade Centre and everyone inside it was, without any doubt, a poorly conceived idea. And yet wasn't it also, in a sense, bringing that vast historical revenge-tragedy between the powerless and the powerful, the poor and the greedy, to the fiery conclusion that leftist intellectuals had long predicted – including during their regular sabbaticals at Yale and Berkeley?

Sure, the fact that the leader of the attackers was a multi-millionaire made it a little harder to sheet the blame home to the obscenity of Western affluence, but not impossible. The most moderate version of the proposition was put by Robert Manne, in the *Age*: the West's 'self-absorption' and 'indifference' to 'Third World needs' has provided 'the ideological soil in which anti-Western and anti-American fanaticism take root'. But apart from failing to explain why the poorest nations in the world have nothing whatever to do with terrorism, the argument also overlooks the fact that, on every economic index available to us, the practical solution to 'Third World needs' is precisely the solution that the Western intellectual left, as well as Osama bin Laden, so bitterly oppose: more globalisation, more cultural and economic connectedness.

And how would Manne's argument explain 'anti-American fanaticism' right here in Australia? When Phillip

Adams informed his Radio National listeners that 'there is madness abroad within the United States', he was talking about the supposed victimisation of Muslims, not the slaughter of thousands of Americans two days earlier. Others chose a more shilly-shallying tack: ie, the supposedly objective discussion of 'why everyone hates America' (they do?) in which one's own hatred of America could be left simmering just beneath the surface. In a copybook example of this genre in the *Age* on September 16, *Eureka Street* editor Morag Fraser managed to denigrate America's view of the world ('myopic', 'banal', 'formulaic'), its leadership ('George W Bush is no force at all'), even its aesthetic traditions ('the world is not a John Ford movie'). But the most extraordinary passage came at the close, as Fraser struggled to find the deep source of America's failings, even as she strained to reinforce her own warm-and-caring credentials:

> On Tuesday night, four hours before the fuel-laden planes hit the World Trade Centre towers, I sat in a quiet Melbourne café reading a book about the fragmentation of American community life … by Robert Putnam … His documented understanding of a great loss – of neighbourliness, of concern for others – in his country would not yield an answer to the bald question, why was America so brutally attacked? But Putnam knows so much about America, and about how America can recover itself, that he has been, for me, prescient consolation in a terrible time.

Hang on! Were the deep networks of 'neighbourliness' and 'concern for others' in American life – networks that of course discountenance the whole argument about the open society's being fatally 'alienated' – ever more obvious and visible than in the days following September 11? Where but among the compassion-mongering Australian intelligentsia could one find such a tin ear for genuine human feeling?

At no point has the chasm between the intelligentsia and the mass of the Australian population seemed wider. Australians love to barrack against the US in any sporting contest (which the intellectuals dismiss as unreflective patriotism), but the weeks following September 11 showed that, for most of us, culturally speaking, Australia and America are contiguous and cognate, the differences being far less significant than the connections. This merely confirmed, of course, what Australians' demonstrated preferences in film, music, and TV had long suggested. But is there more hallowed ground, for the intellectuals, than the need to 'protect' our fragile culture from the 'foreign' culture of America, through local content quotas, cultural tariffs, and other mechanisms for ensuring that actors, writers, and directors enjoy a steady income?

And so the intellectuals, in Australia and throughout the West, entered a phase of moral breast-beating after September 11 – a very public *agon*. As *Arena* editor Guy Rundle noted, it is 'morally impossible to line up with' the United States, which has been responsible for more human suffering than fascism, Nazism, and Stalinism combined. In other words: better to blame America, and by association, ourselves. Some on the left, appalled by this type of madness, (of which there is a plethora of examples in the Appendix), underwent a different kind of *agon*, choosing to abandon their anti-Americanism and rethink their habitual positions: they were duly pilloried, by their former comrades, in journals like *Arena*. But most plumped for an even shriller anti-Americanism, and an even more pointed bourgeois self-hatred, than before: as Peter Saunders writes, 'it did not seem unreasonable, just this once, to break the habit of a lifetime and agree to blame the victim'. If it achieves nothing else, *Blaming Ourselves* will ensure that these people will never be able to step away from the agonised, and agonising, statements they made, that struggled to balance the supposed crimes of capitalism against those of terrorism, and that were so conspicuously devoid of perspective, proportion, and compassion. (Naturally, any criticism of these statements will be denounced as the 'New McCarthyism', but we can live with that.)

September 11 has united the liberal West as it has not been united since the end of World War II. One minor consequence of this unity will likely be the continued withering into irrelevance of the left intelligentsia. For example, in Australia the whole crisis has widened another chasm, the one between the intellectual left, and the mainstream political left: the Australian Labor Party, resisting any temptation to oppose for opposition's sake, has acted throughout the crisis with great honour, and sound judgement. A less minor consequence – and the essays in *Blaming Ourselves*, by their very existence, bear testimony to it – may be the emergence in Australia, finally, after more than 200 years, of a powerful liberal intelligentsia.

Gregory Melleuish *teaches Australian politics, political theory, world history and ancient history at the University of Wollongong. His publications include* Cultural Liberalism in Australia *(CUP, 1995),* The Packaging of Australia *(UNSW Press, 1998),* A Short History of Australian Liberalism *(CIS, 2001) and* John West's Union Amongst the Colonies *(Australian Scholarly Publishing, 2001).*

Imre Salusinszky *teaches English at the University of Newcastle. His newspaper columns have appeared in the* Australian Financial Review, *the* Sydney Morning Herald, *the* Age, *and the* Brisbane Courier-Mail. *His publications include the* Oxford Book of Australian Essays *(OUP, 1997).*

Personal View:
An Australian in New York

Roger Franklin

Twelve weeks have passed since the blue morning of September 11, when the first of two hijacked jets sped so low and loud down the length of Manhattan that my son, who was sitting in a classroom on 28th Street, watched a notice-board shiver on the wall beside him. As he tells the story, his teacher stopped in mid-sentence and then everyone dashed for the windows, overturning desks and chairs in the rush to snatch a glimpse of the anomaly passing overhead. Only the sliver of empty sky between neighbouring high-rises remained. Young Ned, my child, swears that his teacher said 'Something isn't right', and then the class strained ears and imaginations to plot the receding rumble as it faded into the south at 500 miles per hour. A heartbeat later, because the urban landscape

Roger Franklin is an Australian journalist who has spent the past 20 years in the US. Now a senior editor at BusinessWeek, *he has worked for* Time, Fortune, The New York Post *and* Daily News, *as well as contributing to magazines and newspapers around the world. In Australia, his column, Inside America, appears weekly in the* Sunday Age. *He is also the author of* The Defender: The Story of General Dynamics *(Harper & Row, 1986), a critical history of the Pentagon's largest weaponsmith.*

doesn't stand quite so tall on 14th Street, the dog-walkers at Union Square had a better view, able to watch and wonder as the errant jet altered course just a whisker above downtown's water tanks and boxy tenements, the square merlons and cone-capped turrets of the Village skyline. As the shadow and its roar rippled over Canal Street, the World Trade Centre must have filled the cockpit window and the end of some 3,600 human lives was but seconds away.

Today, 160 million tons of concrete and steel, glass, plastic and, yes, thousands of bodies, remain much as they were mounded that day by the hand of an unfathomable evil. With the exception of a single Sunday, when work stopped for a memorial service, the cranes and bulldozers have laboured without pause. According to those who are excavating Ground Zero, working amidst the smoke from fires still burning deep below, better than five million tons of debris have been hauled away. Impressive, indeed it is – but at that rate, it will take five years to clear the site and repair the damage, let alone build a replacement for what was destroyed. Think about it in the terms we New Yorkers now prefer to avoid, not as the exercise in engineering and excavation with which we are comfortable, but on a smaller, human scale: in 2006, when the wives, husbands, partners and children left behind will have had time to seal their grief and perhaps begin again, lost loves and past lives will still be rising like ghosts from the pit.

Not that those remains will be recognisably human. With few exceptions, all the relatively intact corpses were extracted within the first week or so. Then it was parts of bodies, and now, as the dig has gone deeper, mere fragments. It is all a matter of gruesome physics, as a fireman friend who is also a Ground Zero volunteer explained over beers at a neighbourhood bar the other week. Consider the World Trade Centre, he said, as a pair of concrete concertinas that had been stood on end above the deep, steep shafts of their shared foundations. Now, in the mind's eye, collapse the towers once again. Slam down each of the skyscrapers' 100-odd storeys – thump-thump-thump-thump – onto the floors below. At the lowest levels, where many of those who had furthest to descend were caught and crushed almost within sight of safety, that crashing kinetic energy was most intense. As my friend put it, everything and anyone – concrete and flesh – was 'pulped to atoms'.

I have on my desk a four-inch length of steel that testifies to the forces unleashed. Thick as my thumb at one end, it has been drawn out into a curlicue twist at the other, where some terrible strength first teased the metal and then sheared it off in a mirror-shiny, cross-sectioned snip. It is a segment of reinforcing rod, what must have been but a few cells of the ferrous sinews that once stiffened the concrete of the Towers, and I picked it up from the gutter near a gate in the chain-link fence that separates the disaster scene from the rest of this city. I assume that it fell from a truck shuttling to one of the 'sorting grounds' on Staten Island or across the Hudson in New Jersey, where debris is spread by the truckload so sniffer dogs can hunt three-shifts-a-day for human tissue. When such is found, when a frond of fingers turns up or something that might have been a knee is observed within a trouser leg black with blood and soot, the lump is set aside for DNA testing. That is how, chunk by chunk, the dead are being reconstituted, each anonymous element referenced against the bar-coded library of genetic profiles extracted from the relics of the dead – the hair on combs and pillows, even the unwashed socks and underwear that family members surrendered along with the last of their faded hopes.

I beg your indulgence for beginning this way. Believe me, dwelling on the condition of the dead is no mere journalistic device. Why I do so grows from the need to sharpen memories that the mere fact of living in this town has made it necessary – indeed essential – to blur. For those of us who lived through the attacks and must still contend with their aftermath, the urge to edit memories and soften stark images is irresistible.

You see it – or rather you don't see it – on the nightly news. At first, over the initial two weeks or so, the pictures of those planes striking home were everywhere and always. But then, in a demonstration of remarkable restraint, the networks retired their most disturbing footage to the vaults. I can't remember exactly when, for example, I last watched a replay of those cruciform shadows cartwheeling down from the upper floors, each one a human life. We can conceive of a landmark gone missing; it takes an effort, but it can be done. But the mere thought of all those tumbling specks still stops the heart, just as it did to see them on September 11. Now, thanks to the networks' circumspection, we in New York don't have to contemplate the unthinkable – unthinkable even though we saw it happen – unless we so wish. Less than an hour ago, on one of the cable networks' ceaseless gabfests, the producers substituted the most innocuous of computer simulations for the original footage. In this sanitised rendering, a little toy plane brought down bland building blocks. Such visual euphemisms help to push reality back into the more comfortable domain of theory. Everything happened as we saw it, yet we grant ourselves a dispensation not to dwell.

It is that way with so many other aspects of daily life. You might be making your way down a Chinatown street, the sidewalk as crowded and alive as the buckets of squirming, bite-size turtles on sale outside the fish shops, when a capricious gust brings just a whiff, the merest fading scent, of scorched tar and melted plastics. Ground Zero's is a complex stink, sharp on the nose but with so many strange, unknowable taints that it demands real effort to whistle past the graveyard those odours bring to mind. This is the smell of a charnel house, you think. And then, because there is no choice, you exorcise the spectres, force a passage through the throng and continue on your way to dinner with appetite more or less intact.

The 'blitz mentality' is the way Mayor Rudolph Giuliani has described it when urging his city to regain its normal routines. Compartmentalise your thoughts, he counselled. Don't push the horror of that day from mind, but refuse to contemplate the graphic details of that which cannot be undone. Work, consume, pay the mortgage, go out in the morning for bagels if you are a local, catch the Rockettes at Radio City if you happen to be a rube from somewhere else. And when the darkest memories blossom, offer a prayer for the dead and an addendum of private gratitude for the random gift of having been spared.

In the New York of today, this bruised Big Apple of

post-September 11, learning to think that way has become a survival skill. The mental filtering makes it possible, for example, to see my son's classmate, Alicia Fodi, on the schoolhouse steps and not break down at the thought of what happened to her dad. Poor Robert Fodi, Little League coach and devoted father to two other kids, was one of the 350 firemen who died beneath downtown's rubble. For 20 years, he had earned at best a modest living running into burning buildings. At the end, when he was last seen shepherding office workers down the smoke-filled stairwell of Tower One, common sense and instinct must have been screaming that it was madness to remain any longer at his station. Yet he kept at it, staying where conscience and duty ordered until it was too late to save anybody else, including himself. As of a few days ago, no trace of his body had been found.

So here is my reasoning for summoning those images and memories, and for hoping that anyone who reads this – even those half a world away and perhaps many years removed – will forgive my insistent invitation to stare at the massacre's bloody face. I need to do so because, well, the memory of Robert Fodi and his daughter's tears demand as much.

You see, I have spent a good deal of time over the past three months hearing the echoes of September 11 bounce back from places far removed from New York, including my homeland. Muffled by distance, obscured by agenda and almost inevitably steeped in precious self-regard, there have been times when reading the words of those who should know better has been to wade through filth. What we who live here saw, we attempt to soften through the filter of selective memory. As for those who know the massacres only as it was boxed and framed by CNN – the ones who watched the onscreen action through the cold prism of personal prejudice and instinctive anti-Americanism – well, they must have witnessed something else entirely.

For a while, particularly in the weeks prior to Australia's election, it was a daily routine. My computer browser would bring up the latest day's Web pages from Australia's media sites, and there they would be: the latest pronouncement from this salon or that, all different but much the same. Yes, the opinion pieces and commentaries would say, what happened to New York was terrible. But – always that qualifying conjunction – let us not lose a sense of history and perspective. After all, as the scribblers were always at pains to remind lesser minds, this is America that we're talking about, so let's ration and qualify our sympathy. What could those arrogant Yanks expect? They reject the Kyoto treaty and scatter McDonald's amongst the wretched of the earth. They eat too much, talk too loud, and generally act like they rule the world. Who then to blame for the death of Fireman Fodi and so many others?

America, of course!

I'm happy to let this book's other contributors play 'gotcha', to cite the obscene and the absurd, to expose idiocy masquerading as insight, but a few examples warrant exception. There was the snippet, for instance, about the Triple-J staffer in Darwin who jubilantly posted a picture of Osama bin Laden in the newsroom. What could he have been thinking, this toxic simpleton, as he pushed home the last drawing pin? 'There, that will teach those

Yanks!' So, too, with the frequent use of words like 'jingo-
ism' and 'saber rattling', or 'the khaki election', to quote the
on-line Webdiary column of the *Sydney Morning Herald*,
whose editrix and contributors seemed almost to wish that
John Howard would simply drop the pretense and admit
to orchestrating the US massacres as part of some sinister
master plan to secure a third term.

Or what of the letters columns? The polls being
reported in the papers' news pages showed that Australians
were overwhelmingly in favour of sending troops to aid
the US war effort in Afghanistan. Yet not, apparently,
the papers' citizen correspondents. Surely those selecting
the missives for publication couldn't have been weeding
out the ones with which they disagreed? At one stage,
before the effort sickened me and I gave it up, a rough tally
had the letters in the *SMH* running 4-to-1 against Australia's involvement in the campaign against al-Qaeda.

And then, more odious than the rest by an order of
magnitude, there was Phillip Adams in the *Australian*
of October 6. 'Look Back In Anger', the compilation of
misquotations, bogus numbers and selective reasoning was
titled, all deployed in pursuit of Adams's stated goal of
pointing out how America's many sins made it an unfit
friend for Australia. After a pro forma dig at Disneyland
(how original), he proceeded to garble Alexis de Toc-
queville's observations in *Democracy In America* about the
incidence of violence, inflate the number of blacks lynched
by a factor of three and misrepresent the chronology of the
white man's war on the red one, which he says began only
after the colonists expelled the British. Now in full stride,
he overstated the casualties in the Civil War by 60 percent.

Adams blames America – not the UN sanctions nor even Saddam Hussein – for the misery of the Iraqi people. He mentions that Panama City was left 'a smoking ruin' after Bush the Elder's invasion, but not that a homicidal despot was removed and democracy established in the tyrant's place. While nobody, not even Uncle Sam's most adoring nephews, could ever preach the blamelessness of the stern old man with the grey goatee, the fulminating Adams refused to acknowledge that American virtue extended beyond the invention of jazz and the saintliness of FDR. But then any such admissions would defeat the goal of his rant, which was to blame the victim.

It was the same theme that dominated the punditry of *Guardian* columnists, many of whose screeds were dutifully reproduced on Australia's op-ed pages. Almost without exception, they were wrong – wrong about strategy, wrong in their predictions of the course the war would take, wrong about the groundswell of anti-American sentiment they predicted would sweep the Arab world. But no matter, when one pet theory was demolished by events, another hoary old 'lesson' from Vietnam was dragged out, dusted off and served up as received truth. Like generals fighting the last war, the Adamses and the rest had their templates at the ready. Trouble was, only the blind could fail to recognize that, this time, the facts could not be made to fit the form.

From a distance, the heartless might just be able to perceive the Twin Towers as symbols of globalist hegemony. Here though, where we attend funerals and pick pieces of debris – like my twisted paperweight – off the streets of Lower Manhattan, we know different.

War and Terror

The Return to Realism

Owen Harries

Someone – was it Nietzsche? Henry James? Lionel Trilling? – has observed that those who lack the imagination of disaster are doomed to be surprised by the world.

Until September 11 such a lack was very prevalent in the western world. While it was particularly characteristic of US 'liberals', with their belief in progress and perfectibility, it was by no means confined to them. Indeed, in retrospect the emergence of a species of optimistic conservatives – a term that until our time had been close to being an oxymoron – may come to be seen as a distinguishing feature of the last decades of the twentieth century.

In any case, many people of many political and temperamental stripes were taken by surprise by the awful disaster of September 11. That they were was clearly evidenced by the widespread insistence that the acts of terror

Owen Harries is a senior fellow at the Centre for Independent Studies. He taught at the Universities of Sydney and New South Wales, and in the 1970s was head of policy planning in the Department of Foreign Affairs. During 1982–83, he was Australian Ambassador to UNESCO. He was editor of The National Interest, *a Washington-based foreign policy quarterly, from its founding in 1985 until 2001.*

in Manhattan and Washington marked the beginning of a new era, that the world would never be the same again, that everything was changed, and changed utterly.

With all due respect, this was and is nonsense. It reflects not the reality of the matter but the difficulty that intellectuals habitually have in distinguishing between the state of their minds and the state of the world. It also reflects what the philosopher John Anderson termed 'the parochialism of the present', a condition resulting from a combination of ignorance of history and an egotistical insistence on exaggerating the importance of events that more or less directly involve oneself. Horrifying and atrocious as the acts of terror were, it should be remembered that they happened at a time when people who had experienced the Somme and Verdun, the Holocaust and Hiroshima, were still alive.

Far from marking a sharp break with the world in which we have been living for the last decade, this act of terror was an event with which that world had long been pregnant, and there had been many urgent and well-informed warnings of its imminent delivery. Nor were the reasons for such warnings hard to discern. Once the discipline imposed by the superpower rivalry of the Cold war ended; once the authority and control of nation states began to be seriously undermined by transnational and subnational forces; once the movement of people became easy and virtually unmonitored in an increasingly 'borderless' world – and all these things happened in the last ten years – the opportunity for terror increased greatly.

And as globalisation – which is to say, the Westernisation of the world – proceeded rapidly, producing both fear and powerful resentment as it undermined traditional cultures and authority, the motive for terrorism also strengthened greatly.

The point has often been made that terrorism is the weapon of the weak, the losers. In this case these are the elites of some (not all) other civilisations who – on religious and cultural grounds, and because the bases of their authority and power are threatened – furiously reject and oppose the triumph of western ideas, values, institutions and enterprise. Unable either to compete with the West or to hold it at bay, they vent their hatred and despair by terror. Again, the likelihood of this happening was clearly foreseen, notably, though by no means exclusively, by Samuel Huntington.

What happened in September was not that the world changed in some fundamental way, but that in the most dramatic way ideas and assumptions about the world that had come to prevail among large sections of Western elites were shown to be at best inadequate and at worst utterly false. First and foremost there was the assumption that the world was moving rapidly and surely toward a benign, market-driven interdependence; that a positive sum game was in progress in which all would benefit and friction would be smoothed away. With the triumph of the West, too, there came the belief that liberal democracy was destined to triumph rapidly and more or less universally. (As it was I who first published his views, perhaps I should emphasize that this was *not* what was argued by Francis Fukuyama in his famous 'End of History' essay. He allowed for long holdouts against democratisation in substantial parts of the world. Still, the reception given to his views and their subsequent vulgarisation no doubt reflected and contributed to the attraction of the more simplistic version.)

Speaking of simplistic, there was also the complementary belief that traditional power politics had become old hat. As that human weathervane, William Jefferson Clinton, proclaimed, 'the cynical calculations of pure power politics simply does not compute. It is ill-suited to the new era'. It was asserted that 'geoeconomics' had allegedly displaced geopolitics, and that economic wealth and 'soft' power were replacing violence and coercion as the ultimate currency of 'the global village'.

There was, too, the long-standing 'liberal' belief, given a new lease of life by the end of the cold war, that enmity between peoples was the result of misunderstanding and ignorance rather than of genuine conflicts of interests. Once these were removed by education and increasing contact in a multicultural world, it was assumed harmony would prevail.

In the United States the ideas outlined above usually go under the label 'Wilsonianism', after the president who vigorously promoted them. They are not, then, exactly newly minted and, indeed , they were already pretty shop-soiled when Wilson took them up. The 'universal interdependence of nations' was proclaimed by Marx and Engels in their *Communist Manifesto* of 1848. And long before that the belief that proximity and interaction would promote harmony was sufficiently prevalent for Rousseau to feel obliged to contradict it, observing of the states of Europe in the eighteenth century that their condition was such that they 'touch each other at so many points that no one of them can move without jarring all the rest; their variances are all the more deadly, as their ties are more closely woven'. As for the alleged obsolescence of power politics, that is a belief that was widely subscribed to a century ago, on the eve of the Great War.

At a time when American faith in these ideas has received a body blow, it is worth bearing in mind the remarkable durability of such notions. Unfortunately there is truth in the remark that a truly bad idea never really dies, and in Frank Johnson's witty observation that 'Utopia is always an important country, always one of the Great powers'. One can predict with great confidence that these beliefs will survive the present setback and before long will again be advanced as exciting new truths.

But for the immediate future the Wilsonian set of assumptions is not going to be convincing or useful. The belief that conflict is due to ignorance and misunderstanding has been exposed yet again for the nonsense it is. (In today's world, no two groups understand each other more fully than the Israelis and the Palestinians, unless they be the Protestants and Catholics of Northern Ireland.) Far from being adequate for dealing with Osama bin Laden and the Taliban, 'soft' power was partly instrumental in creating them; military power of the old fashioned kind, as well as intelligence and technical knowledge which have always been important sources of power, are needed to destroy them.

But if Wilsonianism is at least temporarily discredited, what will replace it? Well, there is another foreign policy tradition that has figured prominently in American history, one that has recently been brilliantly delineated by Walter

Russell Mead. He labelled it the 'Jacksonian tradition', and some historians have taken issue with him for doing so. But what is important in this context is not the label but the substance. The mindset that Meade describes is immediately recognisable and convincing, as that possessed by a large segment of the American people. It is populist not elitist, characteristic more of men who drive pickup trucks and Harley Davidsons than of college professors or journalists. (One of the most moving sights in Washington is that of the mile-long parade of motor-bikes on Memorial Day, carrying leather jacketed, tattooed men and their wives from all over the country to pay tribute at the Vietnam War Memorial. It is usually sparsely attended by the capital's residents and scarcely written about by journalists.) It is a mindset that is unabashedly patriotic and American-centred rather than cosmopolitan. It regards honour as important and is unforgiving toward those it considers to have behaved dishonourably. It suffers not at all from a sense of guilt or angst. It does not subscribe to the view that truth and morality are relative concepts.

Jacksonianism is normally preoccupied with American domestic affairs and is reluctant to get involved abroad. But once circumstances force it to become involved it is determined to prevail, and is prepared to be ruthless in order to do so. It is prepared to bear pain for the sake of causes it believes in, and to inflict it. As Meade puts it, 'Jacksonians see war as a switch that is either "on" or "off". They do not like the idea of violence on a dimmer switch'. Jacksonians do not think much in terms of exit strategies or negotiated peace settlements.

People of this persuasion and temperament are not

necessarily callous or cruel, but as between humanitarian obligations and the security of their country they have a clear sense of priorities. They would readily subscribe to the view of things once enunciated by Dr. Johnson: 'If a madman were to come into this room with a stick in his hand, no doubt we should pity the state of his mind; but our primary consideration would be to take care of ourselves. We should knock him down first and pity him afterwards'.

This 'Jacksonian' way of looking at things obviously has its limitations. It is not very suitable for dealing with genuine complexity and ambiguity, for it is a view of the world that has little patience for the color grey. On the other hand it is invaluable for cutting through a lot of cant and prevarication and indispensable when there is in fact a straightforward conflict.

It is a way of looking at America's dealing with the rest of the world that was not over-represented at the presidential level in the twentieth century: Teddy Roosevelt, Harry Truman and Ronald Reagan – until now that has been about it. But one senses that this tradition may be well represented in this Bush administration. Indeed, given his Texan background and what we know about his thinking, the President himself may adhere to many of its precepts and assumptions.

And it may be that the tradition is even better represented in the person of Rudy Giuliani. One certainly hopes that his rejection of a donation from a Saudi prince that came accompanied by an offensive sermon represented the authentic mood of the country.

Some would say that it does not. Writing in the *New*

York Times in mid-October, for example, Maureen Dowd maintained that a people who until a few weeks ago had lived in 'a paradise of trivia, wallowing in celebrity, consumerism and cosmetic surgery' now inhabited 'a paranoia of trivia', as the fear of envelopes containing white powder spread. Perhaps. But observing America from a great distance – which may not altogether be a bad thing at a time like this – it seems to me that such a judgement sells the American people short. The citizens of New York – a city that embodied the culture of celebrity and consumerism more than any other – responded to the events of September 11 in a way that did not suggest that they had been fatally enfeebled or rendered paranoid by having lived trivial lives. Having observed the *modus operandi* of the American media at close quarters for 18 years, I suspect that the anthrax 'panic', being a good story, was seriously overplayed.

I believe that the American people have grasped the enormity of the insult that the United States has suffered. They have registered the unrelenting hatred of America that gave rise to it, which in turn has generated a visceral and implacable demand not only for justice but for revenge, and not only toward the particular terrorists responsible but for destroying the will and capacity of international terrorism generally and all who help sustain it. They recognise that negotiation and compromise are not options in dealing with fanaticism, that they amount to nothing but an appeasement that is bound to fail.

If this mood is sustained and this resolve holds, what will have happened will not be so much the entry of America into a new era but the end of a brief pause when euphoria and illusion flourished. It will mean a return to an older, more sober, and above all more realistic state of mind about the world.

Just War after September 11

Sam Roggeveen

The very notion of a 'just war' will sound perverse to some, but on reflection most of us would agree that some things are worth fighting for, and that once we decide to fight we must do so in a morally acceptable way. The Christian just war tradition goes back to St Augustine in the fifth century, and over time has been debated, refined and, in the nineteenth and twentieth centuries, secularised in various documents of international law, most notably the Geneva Convention. Its basic principles find wide agreement across national, cultural and religious divides:

> Justification: Force should only be used in
> self-defence or in defence of a neighbour.
> Discrimination: Force should be directed only
> at those who are attacking you.

Sam Roggeveen *has written on ethics and war for* The Australian Defence Force Journal *and* The Canberra Times, *and has contributed to* Quadrant *and* Policy. *He has a Masters degree in international relations from La Trobe University and was an assistant lecturer in international relations and defence studies at Deakin University.*

Proportionality: Use only as much force as necessary.
Humanity: Treat the enemy and innocent parties with dignity.

Yet the history of warfare in the twentieth century is a history of the steady erosion of these principles, with the terrorist strikes of September 11 being the latest but by no means most egregious example. Nevertheless this essay makes a hopeful argument. It examines not September 11 as such, for the moral case against using innocent civilians in jet planes to kill more innocent civilians in buildings is incontrovertible from the just war perspective. So there is less to say about the attacks themselves than about the ethics of the US-led response. Given the pace of current events I will refer only occasionally to the current campaign, but up to the time of writing it seems to be following a pattern established in the 1991 Gulf War, and repeated in Kosovo in 1999, which will be the primary case studies here.

Indeed this essay argues that the Gulf and Kosovo campaigns signal a hopeful moment in human affairs. Throughout the last century unprecedented effort has been directed at finding more efficient means to kill huge numbers of our fellow human beings, but we have now begun to reverse the trend toward ever-greater destructiveness in war.

The principle of discrimination says that it is morally improper to attack the innocent, even if it serves a greater good. It was the 'greater good' argument that served as President Truman's justification for the bombing of

Hiroshima and Nagasaki. The alternative was to invade the Japanese home islands, which could have cost hundreds of thousands of Japanese and Allied lives. So when the scales were compared it was thought better to sacrifice perhaps 100,000 Japanese civilians now than perhaps five times as many Japanese and US soldiers later. It was this cost accounting in human lives that led the philosopher Elizabeth Anscombe to protest when Oxford conferred an honourary degree on Truman. Anscombe's short essay on this subject ('Mr Truman's Degree') remains one of the most arresting and profound justifications for the maintenance of humane standards in war. Her argument was that although the industrialised nature of modern warfare made it difficult to draw the line between those directly involved in making war and those not, this was not to say that there was no line at all. It is morally obvious that a five-year-old child or an aged grandparent living in Hiroshima had no role in the Japanese war effort, so killing them in order to speed the end of the war was a criminal act.

It might be said that in the age of precision-guided weapons, just war morality has, in Western armed forces at least, gained the upper hand over utilitarian justifications such as those of President Truman. In fact the military historian John Keegan has referred to the Gulf War, in which smart weapons came into relatively widespread use, as 'the first genuine triumph of just war morality since Grotius had defined its guiding principles … in the seventeenth century'. Keegan was making a broad argument concerning the moral justification for the war on the Allied side, but he surely also intended to say something about the manner in which the Allies fought. Technology made it possible to attack targets with great precision, thereby reducing the risk to innocent civilians. It is true, of course, that the vast majority of munitions used in this war were of the old 'dumb' variety, but from a moral perspective what matters is that the Allies went to great effort to minimise collateral damage.

It is also worth noting that in many ways the Gulf War marked merely the start of what has become known as the revolution in military affairs (RMA). Advocates of RMA argue that information technology is putting an end to the industrial age of warfare. At its most extreme RMA suggests a future where wars are fought largely by remote control, with targets (including information nodes) being attacked by computer viruses. In the immediate future RMA promises something rather more familiar — targets will still include troops and physical infrastructure, and these will still be destroyed by high explosive. But the means of delivering these weapons has been revolutionized through precision guidance. The point here is that while critics of Allied action in the Gulf point to how traditional (or 'industrial age') it was in many respects, the war served as a harbinger — the undeniable trend in Western armed forces (since confirmed by US operations in Kosovo and Afghanistan) is toward precision-guided weapons.

Although precision-guided weapons make it is easier to conduct a just war, it is doubtful that the US embarked on an expensive program of rearming itself with smart weapons and pilotless reconnaissance planes for anything other than military reasons. For one thing, though precision guided weapons are expensive, you need far fewer of them, and you also minimise the exposure your forces get to enemy defences if they don't have to bomb a single target over and over. Clearly the primary motivation behind US military transformation has been a desire to fight war more effectively and efficiently; that this has led to a more just means of fighting seems to be secondary. But if the motive for fighting more justly is strictly utilitarian, why wouldn't the US move away from fighting justly for the same reasons? At the beginning of World War II the just war principle of discrimination was fairly well entrenched; the Nazis were the first to break this taboo with their air raids on UK population centres, and soon enough British and then American airpower was put to the same use over Germany, though on a much larger scale. So there is no reason to suppose that just war principles will not be abandoned again if it becomes too costly or too difficult to abide by them.

But precision-guided weapons make it harder to conduct the kind of bombing which destroyed Dresden and parts of London. At present the US still has large stocks of 'dumb' bombs, and has used them to great effect in Iraq, Kosovo and Afghanistan against troop concentrations – such weapons could easily be turned against cities. But by historical standards the US has very few such weapons left, and indeed it is difficult to see that, short of using nuclear weapons, the US would be capable of flattening several whole cities the way it did in World War II – precision-guided munitions are simply not suited to such use.

Another genuine concern among sceptics regarding the moral benefits of the RMA is that making wars less bloody will only make politicians more eager to fight. There is no easy way to prevent leaders from succumbing to such temptation, but what is the alternative? Do we leave troops in the front line or keep using piloted bombers even if a technological substitute is available, just so that a politician will be deterred from going to war by virtue of the risk to that soldier's or pilot's life? That is the moral equivalent of strapping a toddler to the bumper bar to deter reckless driving. What is more, this kind of deterrent has never worked before, and there is not much reason to suppose that human nature has changed so drastically that it would work in future.

But the debate about ethics in modern warfare is more than just technological. It begs broader questions about the nature of war in the twenty-first century, and what the traditional virtues of the fighting man can mean in the age of long-range, precision-guided weapons. John Keegan refers to these virtues as 'honour'. And perhaps critics were alluding to honour when they protested that by bombing Serbian forces from 15,000 feet, NATO was not putting on a fair fight. In support of this claim it is surely true, as Keegan points out, that we naturally feel remorse at having defeated a vastly weaker opponent, because in doing so we know that we have put nothing of ourselves at risk. Keegan takes this as evidence that, just as in sport, combatants prefer a contest between equals in which they can 'glory in victory if they achieve it, acquiesce in honourable defeat if they do not'. Mind you, Keegan seems to see the limitations of the sporting analogy. He recognises that, in the present age, war and the individual have largely 'parted company', in the sense that it is no longer a pure test of physical strength and skill.

There is a more serious weakness in Keegan's

'honour' argument, in that it seems to ignore some contrary aspects of human nature, namely those compelling us to seek out every element of advantage, especially if we know we are in a contest where lives are at stake. It is possible that in Keegan's researches on ancient and primitive warfare, he would have come upon plenty of examples where enemies have indeed honoured the chivalric ideal of a fair fight. But it is surely true in the modern age that no competent commander would surrender technological or other advantages for the sake of a fair fight.

This is what makes the thesis that we have entered a 'post-heroic' age, where commanders are no longer willing to take risks with the lives in their care, problematic. For surely the mentality driving modern policy-makers and military commanders is no different to the mentality of American politicians and commanders of the World War II generation. Is anyone suggesting that if the US had possessed the technological means to overwhelm Germany and Japan the way it did Iraq in the Gulf War it would not have done so? Of course there are many examples of US military commanders who were profligate with the men under their command, but military commanders have generally sought to fight in the most advantageous circumstances – be that by choosing favourable terrain, good weather conditions or superior weapons systems.

Perhaps the comparison with the World War II generation is an unfair one. What if the question asked above were turned around? Let us say the military balance had been roughly the same in the Gulf as that between the US and Germany just before the Normandy landings – would the US have gone ahead with the Gulf War? It is well to point out here that at the beginning of the Gulf War Iraq possessed a huge fighting force equipped with thousands of tanks and artillery pieces – in raw numbers, Iraq outranked the Allied forces in a number of categories. Of course we know now that the Iraqi force was of vastly inferior quality to the Allies, and that the one area where the Allies enjoyed a huge numerical advantage – airpower – was decisive. But none of this was so clear before the war started; that's why the Allies sent thousands of body bags to the Gulf before the fighting began.

So from the Bush Administration's perspective before the war began, decisions on whether and how to use force would have seemed no less momentous or weighty than those which World War II leaders had to make, as they would have been advised that potentially thousands of their own troops' lives were at stake. We can argue, then, that at least in the case of the Gulf War, fear of casualties did not cast an inappropriately dark shadow over military decision-making. But it is true to say that the Allies demonstrably did *not* seek a fair fight. In their use of air power largely to destroy the Iraqi army before the ground war started, the Allies played to their own advantages in their prosecution of the war. This is not evidence of casualty-aversion so much as the prudent use of military force we would want from any competent commander. The US demonstrated such military good sense again in Afghanistan, though the cost to the US of not using its own ground forces was to have to ally itself with morally dubious anti-Taliban forces.

So we ought to applaud the fact that the US values the lives of its soldiers highly, although it could be argued that in Kosovo this concern with friendly casualties came to be the primary aim of the US-led campaign, undermining the ostensible purpose of protecting the Kosovars and punishing Serbia. Indeed, in the Kosovo campaign the judiciousness the US had shown in its application of force in Iraq seemed to give way to outright squeamishness. Of course the US and its allies are to be commended on the fact that, unlike in World War II, they did not flatten entire cities in pursuit of their war aims – this is evidence not of squeamishness but of a just use of force. But what if our war aims demand that we attack a militarily legitimate target knowing beforehand that this will cause the death of innocents? This was NATO's dilemma with regard to Serbia's 'human shields', Serb citizens who voluntarily manned potential NATO targets like bridges, daring NATO to attack. I would not like to have been responsible for such targeting decisions, but surely if these human shields allowed Serbia to further its ethnic cleansing campaign in Kosovo, then the people involved had thereby surrendered their right to be treated as innocent parties. The bridges they occupied could be regarded as legitimate military targets.

In the event, NATO decided not to attack targets carrying human shields, perhaps out of fear of public relations damage. It is difficult to say whether the continued use of the bridges helped Serbia carry out its campaign of ethnic cleansing in Kosovo. But it goes to demonstrate that moral considerations, which need to be made within a robust intellectual framework, can easily be undermined by emotional considerations. The 'softening' of Western society over the last few decades, lamented by some old soldiers, has made us more open to considerations of others' suffering, and has therefore helped us to fight wars more justly. But as the human shields example demonstrates, adopting strict moral guidelines for the prosecution of war involves difficult choices about the degrees and type of suffering we wish to inflict on an enemy, and the softening of society may also have led us to make such choices based more on vague considerations of compassion rather than on rigorous moral grounds. The US will be faced with such choices constantly in its war against terrorism, an enemy so difficult to find amongst innocent civilians.

And so we can be hopeful about the future of warfare. It seems as if the war against terrorism will be fought on the US side in the same manner as the Gulf and Kosovo campaigns – force will be applied in a proportionate and discriminating fashion, without undue cruelty, and with humanitarian care given to innocent parties. Yet despite its hopeful tone, this essay has not been designed to prove the political realists wrong. Realists argue that the structure of the international system, or the eternally corrupt nature of man, will ensure that violent conflict is a staple of international life. We don't have to abandon such scepticism to embrace the idea that we are entering a period of hope in the history of warfare. Nor do we have to say that human nature has been cured of its unsavoury aspects, or that we have somehow mastered the art of politics to the extent that conflict has been banished. As the historian Michael Howard has pointed out, peace in the international system is 'artificial, intricate and highly volatile'. Wars will continue to be fought, but it is apparent that among richer nations at least, they will be fought in more civilised way. Scientific ingenuity has changed the nature of warfare, and much for the better.

'Laden ... bin Laden'

Simon Caterson

[**Editor's note.** The following is an extract from the manuscript of an unfinished James Bond novel of, it must be said, extremely doubtful authenticity. It was discovered, as these things generally are, in a desk drawer among items of furniture and bric-a-brac auctioned at a London saleroom. This episode is the set-piece confrontation between Bond and the criminal genius – in this case 'the Emir', a Middle Eastern terrorist mastermind. The scene takes place in the villain's lair, here a manmade cave hidden somewhere in the mountains of southern Afghanistan. As is the convention, Bond has been captured and, before facing the prospect of a slow, agonising death, only to escape, etc., must engage is a kind of pseudo-intellectual joust with his nemesis.]

Chapter 18
The Perfection of Terror

The sun pulsed in the empty sky like a giant sore, as Bond was half-dragged, half-pushed over rocks and through clumps of thorns. His captors did not speak; their faces

---

Simon Caterson is a freelance writer based in Melbourne.

were as hard and pitiless as the arid terrain.

Bond experienced a surge of nausea. He could feel the blood seep from the wound in his side where the tracking device had been removed a few hours before with an ancient, rusty blade. How had these primitive tribesmen known where to find it or even that such a thing existed?

They came to yet another steep ravine, and Bond stumbled as he began the rapid descent. Through his sun-dazed eyes, Bond noticed something strange. Below a massive outcrop of rock on one side was a giant black rectangle, which seemed to hover in the dust and glare, incongruously symmetrical among the smashed boulders and crazily scattered vegetation.

The shape seemed fixed in space while the landscape lurched around him. Weak as he was, Bond felt compelled to approach it. As they reached the bottom of the ravine the black rectangle resolved itself into the entrance to a cave.

As they passed into darkness, a sudden blast of cold air made Bond feel faint. His knees buckled and he was caught just before his head hit the stone floor, which was almost perfectly smooth.

When he came to, some hours later, Bond found himself lying on a mat at the edge of a low underground dome some 200 metres in diameter exactly opposite the rectangular entrance. The air was cool and he heard a distant humming. The ceiling was covered in dozens of randomly placed light bulbs of varying intensity, like a piece of night sky that had broken off and crashed to earth.

The only other sources of light in the cave were a row of computer monitors along the wall 45 degrees to

Bond's left. To his right, diagonally opposite the computers, was a large screen onto which was being projected a satellite television news broadcast showing footage of bombed villages and wind blasted plains with refugee camps. Seated before the screen were the group of men who had brought him here, but they were now sitting in wonder, completely entranced by the images dancing in front of them. Bond was not sure if the distant sound of explosions came from outside or was part of the soundtrack.

A movement in the gloom on the far side of the cave caught Bond's eye. He saw a figure glide towards him, a white apparition. As the figure approached, Bond saw it was a tall thin man dressed in a long robe and wearing a modest turban. In his right hand he held a walking stick, but moved with no apparent limp.

As he approached, Bond saw the man's face. He had a long white beard. A perfectly straight aquiline nose divided two deep black pools totally surrounded by clear whites. The unblinking gaze was relaxed and disinterested.

'Greetings Mr Bond of the Secret Service.' The voice was soft, polite, honeyed like that of an English actor-knight, the demeanour that of a cleric, or a don. The Emir, for it was he, knelt slowly beside Bond and passed a tray of stale bread and rancid cheese. 'I do apologise, but it is all we have left now.'

Neither touched the food. Bond examined the man minutely. This is the target, he thought, not another of the seemingly innumerable decoys. But he still found it hard to connect this man with the worst acts of terrorism the world had ever seen. Then he remembered the bodies falling from the skyscrapers and the hopeless voices in the doomed airliners. Bond's resolve to complete his mission was reawakened, and his mind sought ways of escape like an octopus feeling its way around a fish tank.

'You may be wondering why you are still alive. In truth, I was curious to see what sort of man could cause me so much trouble. I am sure it is mutual. No doubt you have seen the photograph of the awkward teenage boy in a party of children on holiday in Switzerland. There I was, despised by the others because of my family's wealth and my physical disability. I quickly realised that I would never fit in. As I grew I began to wander among the universities and libraries of the West. I was determined to create something that will outlast us all. My reading led me to the perfection of terror.'

Bond's doubts had vanished. Despite his doll-like passivity, the frail-looking man was true to type: a misfit intent since childhood on revenge against fate and against the world that hated him, or, far worse, was indifferent.

The Emir's gaze had moved to the wall above him. Here it comes, thought Bond, the big speech. 'You alone are privileged to witness the culmination of my life's work. I have dedicated my life to the perfection of terror. I have used my inheritance, to say nothing of my mortal span, solely for this purpose. What I have done will leave no trace of itself, only its effects, and will consume even its creator, but the act itself will never be erased from the consciousness of the world.'

Bond could not remain silent. 'You are just one maniac in a long line of maniacs.'

The Emir paused before replying, but his gaze

remained away from Bond. 'Yes, Mr Bond, I am a maniac. In common with the greatest, most visionary men the world has known. To you, I seem mad. On the other hand, what are you?'

The Emir brooked no reply. 'You are a hollow man, Mr Bond, a man defined and circumscribed by your vices. I have forsworn all the vices of the West, but you are completely controlled by them. Your addictions to women, gambling, alcohol, tobacco, labels, even technology, do these not simply make you the perfect consumer, the perfect slave? You may think you fight for some abstract good, but really this is all you have, all you consist of. Your name should be James Bound.'

'You and your kind are an inchoate mass. It would be easy enough for another man to become you just by adopting your habits, wearing your clothes, driving your car, as I'm sure they do when your job periodically becomes vacant, as again it soon will be.'

'But enough of that. What I would like to explain to you is the theory of terror that led to this. You are the only one who'll know why all this has occurred. They [here he gestured to the tribesmen still transfixed by the screen] are mere instruments, programmed by me to die. As you too will die with me, it is safe to tell you what no one else will ever know. The art of terror, like any high art, must conceal itself. In its purest expression, terror is not a reason or a proof, it poses the one question, in most dramatic terms and there is no answer. It is the sum of all nightmares.'

Bond, who was aching for a cigarette, had never had an aesthetic thought in his life, unless you count an eye for the curve of a Bentley's fender, or the equally enticing shape of a woman's inner thigh. He was incredulous and angry. Most of these lunatics want something to show for their villainy, even if it is just predictable things like power and wealth. They always overreach themselves, but it is never their intention to die. This one was not just crazy, he was insane.

'People who think of terrorism as a political or moral act are only revealing the shallowness of their own imagination. What I have shown them all, though they will never understand, is that terror has an aesthetic dimension so powerful as to be beyond comprehension. People talk of asymmetrical war as if the terrorist is the weaker vessel, but the terrorist is infinitely stronger than his opponent could ever be. If you judge my acts by the effect they have had on the mind of the entire world, then I am the single most powerful man alive.'

'I am not speaking of some empty theatrical gesture, Mr Bond, such as the Easter Rising or the futile killing of a few athletes. What I have in mind is the harnessing of the sublime. I long ago realised that the perfection of terror must not just inspire world-wide fear and panic but also awe. This came to me when I read Edmund Burke.'

Bond had expected the Emir to invoke Bakunin, or some other anarchist crackpot, or even to quote from some fanatical religious tract. But Burke? How could you read Burke as a guru for terror? Despite his loathing for the man, Bond fought to stifle his curiosity.

'I am referring of course to his essay on the sublime and the beautiful, written when he was a young man and before his mind shut down and he became just another apologist for the status quo. It gives me such satisfaction that the things on which the West prides itself most are the things that will most readily destroy it. Inevitably the West supplies, at a competitive rate, the key to its own destruction, it cannot lie about its own rotten heart. Let me quote you my favourite passage.'

He raised a thin finger, and half closed his eyes as he recited. 'No passion as effectively robs the mind of all its powers of acting and reasoning as fear. For fear, being an apprehension of pain or death, operates in a manner that resembles actual pain. Whatever therefore is terrible, with regard to sight, is sublime too, whether this cause of terror, be endued with greatness of dimensions or not; for it is impossible to look on any thing as trifling, or contemptible, that may be dangerous.'

The Emir paused, like a university lecturer quietly waiting for the pens of his students to catch up. 'From this we see that the perfect terror is one in which the actors themselves are mute agents of destruction. They leave no trace of themselves, certainly no explanation of their deed, which in any case they are not capable of understanding. The men who piloted those aeroplanes were superhuman, Mr Bond, because they had no fear of death but embraced it. Since they were children they have been preparing for that moment. Contact with the West gave them not only the skills and the means to complete the task, but, most importantly, it deepened their desire to die. The addictions to which you have succumbed induced in them intolerable feelings of self-loathing. These are men who rushed to death with minds that were clean.'

'As for their targets,' he continued, 'people will think I chose those buildings because they represent Western capitalism or militarism or for some other petty reason which their tiny minds can grasp. Not so, Mr Bond. I chose them because they were *magnificent*. In this Burke guided me, for he tells us that "To the sublime in building, greatness of dimension seems requisite; for on a few parts, and those small, the imagination cannot rise to any idea of infinity". I could go on, but you saw the size of the fireballs and specks of those leaping from the flames. It was a spectacle that will defy all attempts to re-imagine it. The space left by those towers will never again be filled.

'So you see Mr Bond, we two here share this knowledge, so dangerous that it will soon destroy us as surely as those to whom my theory has been applied. Are you ready to die Mr Bond?'

Bond snarled, 'I may die, you bastard, but I will not give up fighting. You think the West is in awe of you, but there is a war going on just outside this cave. You forget about the pilots and passengers who fought the hijackers while knowing they would crash. They will be remembered, even after you and your brainwashed cronies have erased yourselves from the world.'

But the thudding of bombs landing nearby had become louder and the lights in the artificial night sky flickered. The Emir attempted to rise but was too weak to stand. The octopus in Bond's mind kept its steady probing course. The only way to break the spell cast by this clever but infantile man was to demystify him, expose him as the heartless pseudo-intellectual that he was. Bond's mission, he was horrified to realise, was to keep this creature alive, even at the cost of his own life.

Reflections on Violence

Peter Coleman

> Sorel sought to evoke the sublime and
> unleashed the beast.
>> *Guido de Ruggiero*

> It is terrible to kill – but not only others,
> we also kill ourselves when it becomes necessary.
> Because only with violence is this murderous world
> to be changed, as every living person knows.
>> *Berthold Brecht,* The Measure

The corrupt response of so many apologists for the mass murders of September 11 is a product of several influences, ranging from visceral anti-Americanism to the sort of debased common sense that takes the success of terrorism for granted.

One neglected influence is the apocalyptic tradition

Peter Coleman was for 20 years editor of Quadrant. *His books include* The Liberal Conspiracy *(Free Press, 1989);* Memoirs of a Slow Learner *(Angus and Robertson, 1994);* The Heart of James McAuley *(Wildcat Press, 1980) and* Australian Civilization *(ed.) (Cheshire, 1962). He has served in the Commonwealth and NSW Parliaments and was Leader of the Opposition.*

that welcomes the cataclysmic destruction of decadent civilisation. This may be a religious vision (the Book of Revelations) or it may be some variation of a cyclical philosophy of history (Vico). It may be existentialist (Merleau-Ponty's *Humanism and Terror*) or postmodernist (Hardt and Negri's *Empire*) or fundamentalist (Osama bin Laden's Declaration of War against America) .

But one of its most significant visionaries in recent generations has been Georges Sorel, especially in his famous *Refléxions sur la violence*. What has given him authority is that, far from being a simple man of violence, he was an apostle of tradition, law, civility and morality. It may therefore be useful to reexamine his work for the light it casts on the current of ideology that purports to justify or explain terrorism or the 'necessary murder'.

Sorel was born in Normandy in 1847 and studied engineering at the *Ecole Polytechnique* in Paris. He served in the provinces in the department of main roads for more than 20 years, becoming Chief Engineer with the rank of *Chevalier* of the *Légion d'Honneur*. In his late 20s he set up house with his common-law wife, a devout and almost illiterate peasant to whom he was devoted. He became increasingly preoccupied with the decadence, luxury, immorality and venality of France (and indeed Europe) as he experienced it under the Second Empire and the Third Republic. It was a preoccupation that he shared with Baudelaire and Flaubert, and more broadly with Ibsen and Carlyle and most Victorian sages and moralists. Was it for this, he asked, that Themistocles defeated Xerxes at Salamis? Was this why ascetic monks saved Western culture in the Dark Ages? Wherever he looked he saw a contemptible moral emptiness that could command no assent from anyone with any sense of civilisation.

His first books, published while he was still an engineer, were studies of the ancient world, of the decline of Greek civilisation and the rise of Christianity. They are a key to his basic ideas. His *Contribution a l'étude profane de la Bible* (1889) was the first of a life-time's publications on religion, and announced his continuing themes: the Bible as an initiation into the heroic life; the moral grandeur of the early Judaic faith; the importance of miracles in the understanding of Christianity; and contempt for optimism, modernism and the encyclical *Rerum Novarum*.

His second book, also of 1889, on the life and death of Socrates – *Le procès de Socrate* – is a barely disguised attack on French intellectuals. For Sorel, the preservation of Athenian [read, French] traditions, religion and family, even at the price of xenophobia, was overwhelmingly preferable to a Socratic undermining of the values on which the *polis* depended.

But these early books are only a tentative beginning of Sorelian doctrines. The issue that catapulted him into public life was the Dreyfus case. An ardent Dreyfusard who was one of the first to sign the famous Manifesto of the Intellectuals, Sorel saw the persecution of Alfred Dreyfus as symbolising the decay of French justice and honour, and their betrayal by the very forces that should uphold them – the Church and the Army.

Yet he was soon disenchanted with the Dreyfusards and came to believe that they were less interested in justice than is using Dreyfus as a bandwagon for winning political power. The *affaire* finally summed up for him the inescapable cynicism of democratic politics, whether radical or conservative. Now the Sorel of legend began to emerge. Convinced that nothing would come of the political parties and their game of ins and outs, he turned away from Parliamentary politics in his search for sources of renewal.

What was needed, he came to believe, were not the loudmouths of patriotism or justice or the opportunistic reformers but *moral secessionists* – that is, a movement totally contemptuous of corruption, demagoguery, affluence, permissiveness, vote-rigging, protectionism, wheeling and dealing, and all the moral squalor of contemporary France.

Such heroic secessionist movements occur rarely but, if they emerge at all, it is usually at moments of moral and political collapse – such as Sorel observed at the beginning of the twentieth century in France. Primitive Christianity with its apocalyptic belief ('myth') of the Second Coming, was one such example in the ancient world. Another were the monastic orders in the middle ages which in the view of Machiavelli had saved Christianity from total destruction. Yet another were the puritan sects in the early modern period.

With deliberate provocation Sorel characterised these movements as committed to 'violence' – by which he did not mean criminal assaults on people or the destruction of property but an austere and irreconcilable separatism that would culminate in the total social, moral and political transformation of the established order. In the same paradoxical spirit he called his thoughts on these matters 'reflections on violence'.

He took his rejection of reformist rationalism still further. His preoccupation with moral secession led him to his doctrine of heroic myths. We will never understand the transformations of history, he said, by concentrating on the reason or argument of the professors or sociologists or politicians. The key to these movements are the apocalyptic myths drawn from the Bergsonian depths of the soul, the *élan vital*, that sustained them.

The primitive Christians, for example, could not have maintained their historic secessionist unworldliness if they had not profoundly, however irrationally, believed in the imminent return of the Saviour. Are there any movements today, Sorel asked, that offer a comparable hope for the regeneration of our civilisation debased by democracy? For a few years early in the twentieth century Sorel looked to the emerging revolutionary syndicalists. They despised equally the opportunists of the parties and the breezy, compromising wheelers and dealers of business. They upheld the ethic of producers without the manipulative advice of 'our political clergy'. They believed in morality, the family, and ancestral *patrie*. They despised permissiveness, pacifism and feminism. They were utterly indifferent to the charge of being rednecks. The best guide to their values is the work of the anarchist peasant Proudhon. Above all they were sustained by the improbable idea – the myth – of a cataclysmic general strike at some vague time in the future that would transform the world.

Sorel believed that his analysis was a development of Marxism. He dismissed Marx's attempts at economic doctrine or economic history as worthless. (Marx never finished his *Capital*, according to Sorel, because he realised its basic errors.) But Marx's theory of the coming cata-strophic revolution was fruitful – understood not as science but as 'social poetry'. Sorel in this respect antici-pated Marx's most recent biographer Francis Wheen, who in his *Karl Marx* (1999) interprets the Marxian revolution in *Capital* as 'a work of the imagination: a Victorian melo-drama, or a vast Gothic novel'. Sorel saw the second last chapter, in which Marx described the coming revolution, as an epic vision that would have the sort of existential or ennobling effect on the syndicalists or workers that the myth of the Second Coming had on the first Christians.

But Sorel was almost as quickly disenchanted with the syndicalists as he had been with the Dreyfusards, and for similar reasons. The syndicalists, who had once seemed to be agents of regeneration, soon became the mercenaries of political operators hungry for office. The working class was not betrayed. It betrayed itself. It was more interested in working less for more pay than in revolutionising a rotten social system.

Sorel never again found a movement that offered so much promise. He turned his attention briefly to the resurgent French monarchists whose scorn for democracy rivalled his own, but they seemed to be a doomed sect. He also took a continuing interest in the resistance to mod-ernism or 'social catholicism' in the French church, but World War I intervened with its intimation of a new era of barbarism.

Two movements ignited some flickers of hope. One was Bolshevism with its intoxicating (to Sorel) slogan: 'Death to the Intellectuals!' and the other was Mussolini's fascism. But Sorel died in 1922, at the end of his tether ...

and without readers.

What survived of a prolific *oeuvre* over 30 years was not his day-to-day political enthusiasms and disenchantments but his doctrines of decay and regeneration – his revision of Marx and Vico. He was neglected in the years between the Wars. The left could not accept his conservatism and the right could not forgive his enthusiasms for the left. There were occasions when each side considered how best to exploit his name for propaganda. In the early 1930s, for example, representatives of both Stalin and Mussolini sought permission from Sorel's executors to erect a statue on his neglected grave. The executors refused both requests. Whatever their reasons, they made the right decision.

But his main influence was still to come. In the 1960s the New Left and the counter-culture both revived Sorel's ideas of secession. The attack on affluent consumerism echoed Sorel's scorn for a hedonist society that had lost any sense of moral grandeur. The anarchist dismissal of rationalist planning evoked the Sorelian myth. But above all his idea of violence directly and indirectly influenced the new liberationist movements in both the Third World and the West. In particular Sorel heavily influenced Frantz Fanon, whose glorification of existential violence, his call for 'a collective catharsis' of colonial peoples, was popularized in Yasser Arafat's *The Revolution and Violence*, and led directly to Osama bin Laden's creed of terror as being in itself therapeutic.

A moralist like Sorel, whose quest for social regeneration compelled him to sympathise with movements as diverse as syndicalism and royalism, Bolshevism and fascism, would not have been indifferent to the appeal of Marxist Maoism or Islamic fundamentalism or Third World revolution. As his certainty deepened that the West was corrupt beyond internal sources of revival, he looked increasingly to external influences, including barbarism, that might revive it. Part of Russia's appeal to him when he wrote his *Plea for Lenin* in 1919 was its barbaric, its almost Asiatic foreignness. In the same spirit, Jean-Paul Sartre found hope in the Algerian revolution and Michel Foucault in the Iran of Ayatollah Khomeini.

But however much Sorel may have responded to a range of violent movements, it is almost certain that he would have abandoned them as he had the earlier vehicles of his enthusiasms. He would have despised the New Left's mindless demonstrations, sabotage and terrorism. He would have abominated mass murder. He would certainly have condemned the drug cults and the permissiveness of the counter-culture. The point, however, is that this very conservatism, even fastidiousness, adds weight to his continuing influence, making it even more contagious and dangerous.

The New Left and the counter-culture soon lost their *élan*, but the revival of interest in Sorel did not fade with it. In France a *Société d'Études Soreliennes* was formed for the study of his large range of books and essays, not only on politics but also on philosophy, science, and theology. A *Cahiers Georges Sorel* also helped ensure his continuing presence.

His teachings have continued, directly or indirectly, to fertilise the thinking of revolutionaries throughout the world, including terrorists. His secessionism, however 'heroic', justifies any assault on civility. However much he may distinguish his existential doctrine of violence from terrorism, it too has served to justify criminal brutality. Despite all his qualifications, the line runs from Sorel, to Sartre and Fanon, and to Pol Pot and Osama bin Laden.

This is the heart, the evil centre, of the mystery. There were two Sorels. One had a profound, sensitive and conservative sense of civilisation. The other, who has had the greater influence, was a dilettante of violence who championed, however briefly, those violent causes that only deepened the decadence that disgusted him. The ambiguous tone of the title of his most important book encapsulates both tendencies. It is *Reflections on Violence*. He was both a man of reflection and an apologist for violence. As the most famous avatar of this portentous mix, he has contributed to the 'understanding' of September 11.

The rest of us may learn from the conservative Sorel only by being sceptical of the revolutionary. There is nothing epic about conservatism, liberalism and civility. When they are strong, they have the strength of scepticism. It is possible, and desirable, to undertake a *décomposition* of Sorelianism — to reinterpret his separatism as pluralism, his violence as independence, and place them in the context of his ethic of creativity and the rights of producers. Rather than explore or seek heroic myths, a Sorelian would be better advised to return to Sorel's first book and resume his programme for the study of the Bible as the epic of the people and as an inoculation against revolutionary ideas.

But this would remove any lingering apocalyptic appeal of such mystagogues as Lenin or Osama bin Laden.

If Mussolini liked to boast, 'Georges Sorel was my master', there is more wisdom in the advice of Sorel's old syndicalist collaborator, Victor Griffuelhes: 'I no longer read Sorel. I read Dumas'. If you want heroism, *The Three Musketeers* is less dangerous than *Reflections on Violence*.

Our Plague

Douglas Kirsner

> From now on, it can be said that plague was the concern
> of all of us. Hitherto, surprised as he may have been by
> the strange things happening around him, each individual
> citizen had gone about his business as usual, so far as this
> was possible. And no doubt he would have continued
> doing so. But once the town gates were shut, every one
> of us realized that all, the narrator included, were,
> so to speak, in the same boat, and each one of us would
> have to adapt himself to the new conditions of life.
>
> *Albert Camus*, The Plague

There are so many assumptions we take for granted in
living our ordinary life. We won't be attacked randomly
or arbitrarily; we can depend on others respecting our
physical and mental space. We expect to be able to pursue
our normal aims without fear-inducing intrusion. Sure, we

Douglas Kirsner *is senior lecturer in philosophy and psychoanalytic
studies at Deakin University. His most recent book is* Unfree Associations: Inside Psychoanalytic Institutes *(Process Press, 2000). He
was a prominent student activist during the Vietnam era and was
co-editor of* Australian Capitalism: Towards a Socialist Critique
(Penguin, 1972).

need fairness and equality but most of all we depend on others not to harm us in our lawful pursuit of our goals. The first duties of society are the protection of the society itself from attack from within and without, as well as the closely related protection of individuals from each other. Society sets the limits on our intrusion into others' space and provides consequences for the infliction of harm. This allows individuals to pursue their activities more or less free from the fear of being arbitrarily harmed. There is, as social and organisational theorist Elliott Jaques argues, fundamental normal trust within the species that other members will not injure them. However, September 11 and its aftermath have brought an attack on our fundamental values, our sense of the right to survive and live in a normal way. A basic level of anxiety around normal activities is developing. Critics of US responses to the terrorist attacks miss the obvious. The attacks were the work of a bunch of fanatical, fundamentalist Muslims who murdered thousands of people whose only crime was to go to work that day. Taken-for-granted activities such as going to work, opening the mail, flying, working in tall buildings, trusting others not to harm us as a matter of course are now increasingly becoming grounds for fear. Especially given the contagion of bio-terrorism, there are many resonances of Albert Camus' 1947 novel, *The Plague*, an allegory of complicity with the Nazis in World War II.

Civilisation has always consisted of what Elliott Jaques has termed 'connected strangers'. We assume a connection with those around us and assume that they will not harm or injure us. We rely and depend on them for many things, but at a basic level we assume that they will not act against us without good reason. We require that our lives be relatively stable and predictable so that we can get our daily tasks done and relax. We assume that murders are for a (misguided) reason and not random, i.e. that specific people are targeted, not everybody randomly.

As communications and technology have grown from local to regional to global, so has the awareness of an increase in major differentials in the quality of life between the haves and the have-nots. Poverty and misery are issues as wide as the normal awareness and the net of communications. The move to the economic and political global village means that global differential economics provide the source of far wider roots of conflicts than in previous ages. The experience of the economic organism, that by doing what we can for some others, we can get back what we want from others, is far from rewarding. It is completely dissonant in Third World countries where the gap between the Third World and the First World is so close in communications yet so distant in the reality of what ordinary people can expect in their lives. Any semblance of First World satisfactions is manifestly unreachable for most ordinary people in the Third World. What adds insult to injury in the Third World is that the First World has done too little to address this growing gap between rich and poor countries in any meaningful way. The global village brings responsibilities for those most well off in that village to help care for those least so. The First World has dismally failed at that task. It should be clear that it is in the interests of the First World to address this crucial issue if the opportunity for terrorists to grow and find adherents is to be reduced. Our fundamental need for protection from injury and harm is thus aligned to our duty to care for others.

World War I was followed by the Treaty of Versailles and humiliation and painful reparations for Germany. The soil upon which Nazism could develop was established. A confluence of factors including the onset of the Great Depression provided the opportunity for the Nazis to prevail in Germany. The Marshall Plan that followed World War II was the product of a far different strategy that helped Europe recover economically and undermine the conditions for a resurgence of mass movements of Nazism and fascism. Both Germany and Japan have succeeded as economically buoyant and healthy democracies. The world has become far more connected since World War II yet the US has forgotten the historical lesson of the success of the Marshall Plan and has ignored the needs of the Third World and often exploited it.

The current war is a struggle against evil. Critics often erroneously assume that this means that those struggling against this evil are therefore supposing themselves to be pure good. The critics then go on to adumbrate the faults in US foreign policy as though this meant we should not fight the other side. But World War II involved an alliance of good and not so good countries such as Stalin's USSR struggling against a manifest menace to humanity. Would it have been right for Britons and Australians not to have fought the Nazis because the British Empire was flawed? Finding fault with the US in its fight against the terrorists is irrelevant in this context, beside the point. It is not so much a struggle of good and evil as a struggle of people of different backgrounds and standpoints against evil. When it comes to evil, bin Laden and his associates trump everybody else around. Stereotypical suggestions of moral equivalence between the terrorists and their associates and the West are highly dubious. As Elliott Jaques has recently argued:

> The basic glue that holds us together, that allows humanity to live together, that is the foundation of the existence of humanity, is the existence of mutual trust that each will not harm the other. To be able to rely upon that bond is the final good. For individuals to decide to break that bond is the essence of evil. Species survival, humanity, is at stake.

Many factors are connected to the attacks. The ground upon which terrorists can thrive like opportunistic infections needs to be addressed as a matter of urgency once this immediate war has succeeded. However, the soil of Third World deprivation provides insufficient explanation in itself. Poverty no more causes terrorism than women wearing miniskirts cause rape. There are many far poorer parts of the world that have not produced terrorism or support for it. Besides, what fundamentalists fear most is modernisation, with its liberal, secular sequelae (sexual equality and freedom, challenges to traditional authority, media, the internet). They struggle mightily against all its manifestations. The attack on the World Trade Centre assaulted American civil society as such – not particular government foreign policies, but the American people, their basic values and form of life: 'life, liberty and the pursuit of happiness'. Such values are fundamental to democracy and progress in many nations around the world, including Australia.

A crucial factor is the involvement of a climate of fanaticism. But not just fanaticism: religious fanaticism – and a specific type of religious fanaticism, Muslim religious fanaticism, what Christopher Hitchens has labelled 'fascism with an Islamic face'. People can be fanatical without imposing their views on others with the force of arms. To enforce their aims, Muslim fanatics insist on using force or acquiring state power and crushing any opposition. Most of the terrorists around the world consist of fundamentalist Muslims on a *jihad* against secularism. Everything else is an excuse. If the House of Saud were to leave Saudi Arabia with every American soldier and Israel were to be driven into the sea, there would still be women wearing bikinis and miniskirts in the West; women employed in responsible jobs, including serving in the military; Jews, Christians, atheists and tolerant Muslims speaking their minds; TV, movies and so many other fruits of modernisation and secular freedom in the modern state that the fundamentalist Muslims view as anathema. They are fundamentally opposed to the separation of church and state, the only 'church' allowed is their extremist version of Islam. For them the Great and Little Satans (the US and Israel) are Infidels who need to be eradicated. The terrorists not only have their own dogmatic self-certain religious beliefs but they insist on imposing them on others at the level of society, law and social structure, and tenaciously oppressing anybody who disagrees with them. Their fixed, fanatical delusional mentalities are incommensurate with any dialogue or negotiation with others of different views.

I believe that those well-meaning left critics of the war have been grossly naïve as to the dangers of not fighting the terrorists. The failings of US foreign policy have no more relevance as to whether we need to struggle against this clear and present danger than did misgivings about our allies during World War II. The Islamic fundamentalist fascists place everybody else in grave danger. They do not play by 'the rules' and will use any means whatever to try and achieve victory. They are fanatics of the most dangerous kind whose division into true Muslims and Infidels is almost identical to the distinction between human and vermin. Sanctioned by their dogmatic delusional ideology that supposedly guarantees them a glorious place in heaven for sacrificing their lives as 'martyrs', they respect no limits and make no distinctions between soldiers and civilians or between legitimate and illegitimate targets. This is not 'normal' warfare by any previous standard – if you blink, you lose.

Leftists have divided on the historical analogies of the present war. Many like Noam Chomsky treat it like Vietnam and are hard-line attackers of the US administration's approach, while a far smaller yet far saner number like Christopher Hitchens see it as like World War II and seek a broad united front against terrorism. But whatever resonances the present anti-war movement may appear to have with the protest movement against the Vietnam War there is in my view no similarity between these wars. The US this time is under attack, not the attacker. Vietnam was a war of foreign intervention by the US in a situation of civil war. The Vietnamese people wanted the right to determine their own government and broadly supported the

Viet Cong. The domino theory was totally erroneous. While the US was involved in an unjust war then, war is not always to be avoided. In my opinion, the analogy is much closer to the events leading to World War II. What can we learn from the mindsets of the late 1930s dealing (or not dealing) with the Nazi threat? Chamberlain's policy of appeasement by sacrificing Czechoslovakia to the Nazis at Munich in 1938 was counter-productive, contributing to the strengthening of Nazi power and resolve. The attack on the World Trade Centre is also a tragic reminder of the omen of *Kristallnacht*, when the Nazis set fire to synagogues and ravaged Jewish-owned shops throughout Germany and Austria. The Chomskyites have allowed the left to be further sidelined, as irrelevant and frankly irresponsible. I remain as convinced by the compelling intellectual reasons for having opposed the Vietnam War as I am by the need to support this one.

Old right versus left stereotypes don't hold up. I have been struck by one glaring local Australian example of just how anomalous such stereotypes are. Whatever the rights and wrongs of illegal immigration, it is inconsistent for many Australian leftists to be, on the one hand, so critical of the fact that Australia turned away many Afghan asylum seekers seeking to land illegally by boat in Australia and yet, on the other hand, oppose the war against the Taliban, who produced the political and much of the economic aspect of the Afghan refugee problem in the first place. If the savagery of the Taliban regime is the cause of desperate measures by many asylum seekers, would it not follow that many more potential refugees could be saved their perilous journey by eliminating the cause of their suffering back in Afghanistan? Focus on the alleged rights of a few hundred illegally to enter Australia has stood in stark contrast to the critics' condemnation of the war on the causes of the need of these refugees (and millions of others) to flee Taliban terror. Victory makes it possible for millions of Afghans to return home as well as for the Afghan population to be freed from Taliban tyranny. This is an incomparably more humanitarian solution than opposing the war and accepting hundreds or even thousands of refugees and therefore leaving the Taliban to rule and having millions of Afghans in Pakistani refugee camps. The joy of the men, women and children welcoming the US/Northern Alliance liberation from the brutality of the Taliban should help such critics realise just how wrong they have been. Only with the liberation have Afghan women been able to go out into the street alone and shed their *burqas*. Protesting against the war has supported terrorism and misogyny.

The terrorist events reminded me of a concept developed by the psychiatrist R.D. Laing in his classic book on psychosis first published in 1960, *The Divided Self*. There Laing described our everyday sense of 'primary ontological security'. The ordinary person most of the time approaches life's hazards from a standpoint of some kind of 'centrally firm sense of his own and other people's reality and identity', relying on the substantiality of natural processes and that of others. On the other hand, the 'ontologically insecure' person is lacking in such certainties, may not possess an over-riding sense of 'personal consistency or cohesiveness' and the person's 'identity and autonomy are always in question'. According to Laing, 'the ontologically insecure person is concerned with preserving rather than gratifying himself: the ordinary circumstances of living threaten his *low threshold* of security'. The world of the ontologically insecure patient described in Laing's work underlines the large extent to which our personal identity is embedded in our social contexts and is a function of them. I think that the terrorist threat to us all brings home how much social events impact on what we take to be normal experiences of personal identity and ourselves, others and society as reliable, real and trustworthy. To an extent, the terrorist threat challenges the reliability of our 'ontological security' and raises the spectre of ontological insecurity as a significant part of our lives. The terrorist threat of arbitrary persecution and lack of reliance on normal verities plunges us into another world where less and less can be taken for granted. The indiscriminate threat of terror (such as anthrax or just going to work in a tall building) can raise primitive anxieties to a threshold that can interfere with and even threaten to dominate our lives. This attack on our security highlights our funda-mental reliance on mutual trust not to harm each other as a base upon which we can get on with our lives construc-tively. The attacks on our security impact on everyday life. In everyday life, as American psychoanalyst Robert Stolorow observed in a 1999 article in *Psychoanalytic Psy-chology*, we unconsciously rely on absolutisms that we do not question and that are not open for discussion, such as somebody saying to a friend, 'I'll see you later', or a parent saying to a child at bedtime, 'I'll see you in the morning'. According to Stolorow,

Such absolutisms are the basis for a kind of naive realism and optimism that allow one to function in the world, experienced as stable and predictable. It is in the essence of psychological trauma that it shatters these absolutisms, a catastrophic loss of innocence that permanently alters one's sense of being-in-the-world. Massive deconstruction of the absolutisms of everyday life exposes the inescapable contingency of existence on a universe that is random and unpredictable and in which no safety or continuity of being can be assured.

The September 11 epiphany and the continuing terrorist threats have wrought this kind of trauma to many.

One reaction to this real threat to our security has been to 'turn a blind eye' to the real threats posed by terrorism. This involves denying the reality and displacing the problems elsewhere. This means avoiding the obvious, that which stands in front of us but which we do not see. One method of avoiding this reality in the present case is to blame ourselves for what happened – our society, the US, etc. – as a way to paralyse ourselves and avoid action against real evil. This can be rationalised as siding with the underdog against First World imperialism, mistakenly making the US responsible for most of the world's ills. They do not take sufficiently seriously the real, destructive role of the anti-human fundamentalist interpretations of Islam that advocate bloodshed against and suppression of other cultures, including those within Islam which do not meet their exacting strictures. The Israeli-Palestinian conflict is also a red herring in this connection except insofar as terrorist organisations such as Hamas and Islamic Jihad are also part of the same problem of attacks on ordinary people by suicide bombers and other fanatical murderers.

This is not the time for *mea culpa*. The terrorists began the war, not the US. If the US does not succeed in powerfully responding by rooting out the terrorist networks, more such attacks on US soil and around the world are certain. It is vital that the US administration takes a strong stand and carries it through. Of course, we need to confront real problems of the disparity between rich and poor nations – but the terrorist networks need to be eradicated first.

This struggle cannot be sidestepped by arguing that the cause of terrorism lies in US policies any more than combating the Nazis could have been avoided by saying the ground for Hitler was laid at Versailles. In *The Plague*, Camus expressed the response well: 'We should not act as if there were no likelihood that half the population could be wiped out; for then it would be'.

Civilisation and Values

The Unusual Suspect: Reflections on the Attack on America

Chandran Kukathas

Even as US authorities began to pursue the available leads to find the perpetrators of the terror of September 11, others had begun to ask whether the enemy really lay within, and it was not long before the usual suspect was produced. That suspect was a shadowy figure whose hands reached like tentacles into innumerable corners of the world. Independent, and wealthy beyond imagination, the suspect, a master of disguise, went by many names: capitalism, the West, modernity – to identify only some of those best known. The suspect's real name, however, is well-known. It is America.

Yet this suspect is really a very unusual suspect. And understanding this might help us to understand why September 11 happened, and what it means in modern

Chandran Kukathas *is Associate Professor in the School of Politics, University College, UNSW at the Australian Defence Force Academy. His main interests are in political philosophy. His books include* Hayek and Modern Liberalism *(OUP, 1989),* The Theory of Politics: An Australian Perspective *(with William Maley and David Lovell, Longmans, 1990) and* The Liberal Archipelago: A Theory of Liberty and Freedom *(OUP, 2002).*

history. For this suspect is not a person, or a group, or an institution, or a people, or a nation, or even a state. The suspect is an idea. For many, it is an exasperating idea, for although it has been found on the scene of numerous crimes, linked to atrocities of all kinds, tried and found wanting on countless tribunals, it has simply refused to be contained, to disappear, or to die. If anything it simply grows stronger. What is this idea?

The idea, which is both revered and reviled, is freedom.

Simply saying the word 'freedom', however, does not get us very far, since the meaning of the term is highly contested. Understandings of freedom are many, and a variety of groups, from communists to republicans to liberals of all stripes, have claimed to be its defenders. For some there can be no freedom where there is poverty, for others there can be no freedom without law, and for many there can be no freedom where there is power exercised by the strong over the defenceless. Even among those who share the same views on such matters, there is disagreement over what counts as poverty, or what is law, or what constitutes the legitimate use of power. When freedom is invoked many nod in assent, but they are often hearing different things – even if not always very different things. The question, however, is what is the idea of freedom that the word 'America' stands for?

America stands for the idea that people should be free to live by their own lights, regardless of the opinions or convictions of others. It is this idea more than anything else that has drawn such a diversity of peoples to the United States over the past 250 years: the idea that people are free to make their own lives. It is not that this possibility does not exist anywhere else, or that the notion that differences may be accommodated is something especially new in human history. But in America it is a point of principle. Its founding documents declare that individuals have rights – including the right to pursue happiness – which may not be taken away by any authority, and that governments may not make laws that prevent them from speaking, worshipping, or gathering freely in pursuit of their own ideals. It is in America that the ideas of toleration of difference, freedom to dissent, and open government find their strongest expression. Out of a turbulent history, in which the idea of freedom in theory struggled to overcome slavery in practice, there developed a legal and political tradition that made individual rights a matter of principle rather than a matter of custom. America did not invent the idea of freedom, or the notion of a right. But it has given these words a vigour they did not always possess. America's reach across the world may be measured by the extent to which these words are now a part of the currency of international moral, legal and political discourse.

Yet at the same time America is not a singular agent or person. It is made up of 50 states with independent legislatures; its many governments face regular and frequent elections (the Houses of Congress go to the people every two years); its President may not serve more than eight years; and lawmakers are bound by a Constitution whose interpretation is the province of an independent Court. The American polity itself is an expression of the idea of freedom for it was constructed in the conviction that power must be separated, divided and contained if individual liberty was to be protected. America is powerful; and within it there are many powerful people. But it does not have a single ruler or a single supreme tribunal. On the contrary, every office holder is answerable to another; and all are, to varying degrees, subject to public scrutiny through the broadcast media and the press. But no officer is supreme. When Harry Truman placed a notice on his desk reading 'The Buck Stops Here' he was being, at best, highly optimistic. In this political system the buck stops at many places, for responsibility is devolved even as those bearing responsibility are scrutinised.

But for many people all this is not only incomprehensible but exasperating. For Osama bin Laden, and for his followers and defenders, what is incomprehensible is the attraction of the American idea: the idea that people should simply be left free to pave their own way to hell, even when they believe they are climbing up to heaven. What must be exasperating is that any effort to disabuse people of their desire for this freedom is usually met by vacant stares. America remains a beacon. (The main motive even of many migrants to Canada, a professor and student of Canadian multiculturalism remarked ruefully to me, seemed to be to get to the United States.)

But for America's Western detractors what is incomprehensible is that people everywhere do not behave in a manner that shows they understand how sinful the American way is. People everywhere consume America's culture as ravenously as they do its fast foods, while imitating its products, using its currency (when their governments have proven financially incompetent or corrupt, as in

Argentina), and copying its laws. People are by instinct capitalists, since they are inclined to accumulate and to trade for profit, and America officially welcomes the capitalist spirit. But America's detractors see in capitalism only greed and exploitation rather than the (risky) opportunity to become independent (sometimes by becoming outstandingly rich).

What these detractors find exasperating, however, is that America does not use its great riches to do more good – to solve problems of poverty or hunger or underdevelopment. Instead, as they see it, American wealth is used simply to expand its influence without any thought given to the wretched. When things don't go well for people in the world, someone must be to blame and America always looks the most likely candidate. When crimes are committed, the source of the evil must be found, and America is always a promising source. It is rich, it consumes far too much of the earth's resources, and gives too little to the world in return.

The attacks of September 11 were an assault on the idea of a modern world of the sort exemplified by America. The effect, without doubt, has been devastating – not only because of the impact on those who lost their lives or lost the lives of others close to them, but because the fear and uncertainty it created has been palpable. Yet what is curious is how small a dint this event has made in the real target of the attacks: America and the idea of America. The reason is not simply that the destruction of the World Trade Centre killed people from all over the world and brought world-wide condemnation of terror and sympathy for the United States. The reason is that the idea being attacked is just too resilient.

Just after the second tower of the World Trade Centre was destroyed, the novelist, Tom Clancy, being interviewed observing these events as they were happening and as more suicide missions were under way, was asked what he thought needed to be done. In a striking passage of commentary, he pointed out that it is at times like this that a society's most important values are tested, and that on this occasion it was American society's capacity for tolerance and respect for human rights that would be challenged. But now more than ever, he suggested, it was important to hold on to those values rather than cast them aside in pursuit of vengeance. The perpetrators must be pursued; but not at the expense of the values which lay at the heart of the American ideal.

In the months that have followed what is remarkable is how much restraint has been shown in pursuing the groups that have sought to wage war on the United States. Every effort has been made not to turn the search for al-Qaeda into a challenge to Islam. Calls for indiscriminate bombing (notably from some American neo-conservatives) have been resisted. But, most importantly, even as Arabs and Americans of Arab descent were being rounded up for questioning, civil rights groups and lawyers began standing up to remind authorities that these individuals had rights, that detention without trial was unacceptable, and that proposals for the establishment of special courts were not acceptable. Individuals still had rights.

It would be a mistake to suggest that America has a stainless moral record in its short history. Its blemishes have been revealed by its own scholars and critics for all to see.

The institution of slavery and the discrimination against blacks, the dispossession of Native Americans, the wartime incarceration of Japanese Americans, have all been roundly condemned by Americans themselves. Its foreign policy failures from Vietnam to Somalia have been dissected in the American academies and in the American media. And its government's occasional lectures to others about free trade and international justice have often rung hollow as American policy in practice has failed to live up to US political rhetoric. It is no doubt these things that America's critics have in mind when they cast it in the image of the world's villain. It is probably all that the fanatical opponents of modernity see when the name of the United States is invoked. But if this were all there was to the United States, the suspect would be an easy target. People would not be sympathetic to such a nation even in such times as these. Nor, more significantly, would they be standing at its borders waiting for green cards.

What is attractive about America is the ideal it embodies. Some have seen that ideal simply as capitalism, or as modernity, or as a collection of Western values. Certainly these are some of the things that America's attackers have in their sights. But none of these notions captures the ideal. Abraham Lincoln came closer when he described America as a nation 'conceived in liberty and dedicated to the proposition that all men are created equal'. In its dedication to liberty it is a nation which is as a matter of principle (however imperfect the practice) willing to allow even those who do not share this ideal a place in society. It is a modern society which insists that there be room allowed for those who reject modernity.

The attacks of September 11 were launched by a group of people who reject modernity, and who see America as its embodiment. The attacks were not inconsequential; and some things may never be the same again. But what ought not to be lost sight of, in the end, is how unsuccessful they were. For the assault on the idea that lies at the heart of modern society missed its mark completely. People will not any time soon be turning in great numbers to Iran or Saudi Arabia for inspiration or guidance. In historical terms, the attacks on New York and Washington were acts of desperation launched by people who could not see that history has passed them by. Modernity is the only real game in town; blaming America is simply the silliest.

Patriotism as the Last Refuge of the Liberal: Fostering harmony in a liberal multicultural society

Andrew Norton

> The cricket test – which side do they
> cheer for? Are you still looking back to where
> you came from or where you are?
>
> *Norman Tebbit, former Chairman of*
> *the British Conservative Party*

The British Tory politician Norman Tebbit wasn't known for the subtlety of his views, on immigration or much else. The member for Chingford was dubbed the 'Chingford skinhead'. Yet his 'cricket test' of migrant allegiance captures one of the questions that multicultural societies

Andrew Norton *is a Research Fellow at The Centre for Independent Studies, and also holds a part-time position at the University of Melbourne. From November 1997 to December 1999 he was Higher Education Adviser to Dr David Kemp, Federal Minister for Education, Training and Youth Affairs. Prior to joining Dr Kemp he was Editor of* Policy, *the quarterly journal of The Centre for Independent Studies. He was an editor and contributor to* A Defence of Economic Rationalism *(Allen & Unwin, 1993),* Shaping the Social Virtues *(CIS, 1994) and* Markets, Morals and Community *(CIS, 1996).*

must face — how to deal with the dual loyalties of migrants.

The September 11 atrocities in New York and Washington, and the commencement of war against the al-Qaeda terrorists and the Taliban regime a few weeks later, again highlighted the problem of potential conflicting loyalties, in the most significant way — not a gentlemanly game of cricket, but a life-and-death contest.

Osama bin Laden and the Taliban have worked hard to portray the attacks on them as attacks on all Muslims, justifying a *jihad* against the West. That message resonates powerfully in neighbouring Pakistan, where at the time of writing there were regular demonstrations against the Pakistani government's support for the war, and men crossing the Afghan border to join the battle. Muslim governments around the world condemned terrorism without supporting any meaningful action against it, realising that parts of their own populations opposed attacks on fellow Muslims, even though Western leaders repeatedly stressed that this was a war on terrorism, not on Islam.

My concern here is not with the stance of foreign governments, but the implications for Australia's own multicultural society. With people here from virtually every nation in the world, almost any military conflict puts some people in the invidious position of having to choose between their country of birth and their country of residence. In 1996 there were about 9,000 people of Afghan birth or descent, but with refugee arrivals since that number would now be higher. In the war on terrorism there is another layer of complexity. The efforts of al-Qaeda and the Taliban to frame this war as one between

Muslims and the West greatly expands the potential number of people who could feel divided loyalties.

The 1996 census found just over 200,000 Muslims resident in Australia, but with births and new arrivals since, the current number would be higher. While there were a handful of Muslim convicts and seamen in the initial settlements, and Muslim camel drivers helped open up the outback, the vast majority of Australian Muslims (or their parents) have arrived over the last thirty years. In 1971 the census identified only 22,000 Muslims, so the population will soon, if it has not already, have increased ten-fold in a generation.

Only a handful of these Australian Muslims have, so far, been associated with overseas Islamist movements. It is useful to distinguish between 'Islamism' and 'Islam'. While Islamists may not be any more religious that other Muslims, they are distinctive in their view of politics. Islamists intertwine the spread of Islam with the creation of an Islamic state, making Islam a form of government as well as a religion. As with other groups believing they act with the authority of God, democratic procedures do not figure prominently among Islamist tactics. A *jihad*, normally an act of self-defence, is redefined by Islamists to allow warfare against anyone who stands in their way, including other Muslims. Islamism is Islam at its most illiberal, completely rejecting the separation of church (or mosque, as the case may be) and state, and imposing Islamic rule on all. The brutal oppression practised by the Taliban regime in Afghanistan is its logical consequence.

In other Western countries, there is cause for concern about Muslim support for Islamist causes, and where this

might lead. Islamist terrorist groups exist in major conti-
nental European countries such as Italy, Spain, Germany
and France. In Britain, the *Sunday Times* published a survey
of British Muslims. A very substantial minority – forty
percent – agreed that Osama bin Laden was 'justified in
any way to mount his war against the United States'. Sev-
enty-three percent did not think Tony Blair was right to
join the United States in its war against the Taliban and
Osama bin Laden. Ninety-six percent said that the US
should stop its bombing of Afghanistan. Significantly, the
first British casualties in the war were not troops, but
British Muslims who had gone to help the Taliban. While
this level of treachery is not yet on display in the United
States, Islamists are resident there. A number advocate
replacing the secular American state with an Islamic state.
In itself, this makes them no more than another of the usually harmless groups of nutters that populate the fringes of
American politics. In the context of September 11, however, it is worrying that supporters of the Taliban's goals are
present in the US.

In Australia, no Islamist terrorist groups have been
uncovered, but the Islamic community is not free of suspicion. Its spiritual leader, Sheik Taj El–Hilaly, has a history of
inflammatory remarks going back to the 1980s, and indeed
was lucky not to have been deported. Most recently,
Andrew Bolt in the *Herald-Sun* reported on unscreened
SBS TV footage of El-Hilaly describing anyone who died
fighting for Islam as a 'hero'. The Australian organisation
with the best documented links to Islamist movements is
the Islamic Youth Movement (IYM), based in Sydney. Its
journal *Nida'ul Islam*, 'The Call of Islam', has run inter-

views with Osama bin Laden and Sheikh Omar Abdul
Rahman, from his US prison cell, where he is serving a life
sentence for plotting the 1993 attempt to blow up the
World Trade Centre, and various other conspiracies, such
as to bomb the United Nations and to assassinate Egyptian
President Hosni Mubarak. *Nida'ul Islam* has also published
crude anti-Semitism. IYM has attracted media coverage
for its 'hunting trips' to a property in southern NSW,
where ASIO found a make-shift rifle range and empty
shells. The homes of IYM members have also been raided.

El-Hilaly's comments were made, and IYM's articles
were published, before September 11, and do not advocate
violence or active support for Islamist causes in Australia.
If they did, they could be committing treason. According
to the Commonwealth Crimes Act, treason includes assist-
ing 'by any means whatever' an enemy at war with the
Commonwealth, whether or not a war has been declared.
The maximum penalty is life imprisonment.

Representatives of other Islamic organisations do not
issue statements supporting Islamist causes or the heroism
of those who die for Islam, but nor do they back the war
against terrorism in Afghanistan. While defensible – if, in
my view unconvincing – arguments can be made against
the war, this stance naturally raises concerns among the
general public about the true motivations of more mainstream Islamic organisations. In 'peace' rallies held in early
November, people billed by the media as representing
Islamic organisations appeared alongside hardcore anti-
Western activists, notorious for the violence and vandalism
of the S11 and M1 demonstrations. Of course agreeing
with someone on one issue does not mean you have

common cause with them on others. But you risk being judged by the company you keep.

In earlier times in Australia this would have been a serious risk. In World War II, for example, the Australian government had significant powers over 'enemy aliens', in those days a person who 'possesses the nationality of a State at war with His Majesty', rather than somebody from another planet. The powers ranged from the seemingly eccentric (prohibiting the possession of carrier pigeons, for example), to politically disabling restrictions on speech and association, to detention for unlimited periods of time. At the peak time, in September 1942, nearly 7,000 'enemy aliens' were detained, the majority of whom were Italian, though all Japanese were interned. Those protesting against the loss of innocent German lives in continued Allied air raids would likely have had their freedom of speech curtailed, or have faced internment.

Even during World War II, in a society far less self-consciously liberal than Australia today, these measures were the subject of public protest. Detention was sometimes imposed quite arbitrarily, carried out by often ill-informed local police. Among those detained were people who had fled European fascism, and were most unlikely sympathisers with the Nazi cause. 'Enemy aliens' were given a right to object, and by late 1944 the number of people interned had dropped below 1,400.

Despite complaints about the 'illiberal' treatment of people trying to become refugees in Australia, the official attitude toward 'enemy aliens' this time around indicates how much more liberal and tolerant Australian politics has become over the last half century. So far as I am aware, internment of those already in Australia has not even been suggested by political fringe groups, much less found its way to the statute books. Nobody is suggesting that freedom of speech be further restricted, and the restrictions that do exist, such as those on racial and religious vilification, protect rather than threaten those who want to participate in public debate on the war. Liberal institutions seem secure in Australia.

The issues this conflict creates, then, are not about the overall legal framework. Rather, they are about how we manage the tensions likely to arise within the Australian community when parts of it are perceived by others as being complicit with an enemy. The number of Australians seriously hostile to minority ethnic or cultural groups is probably quite small. In the late 1990s only 6 percent of the population thought multiculturalism had been 'very bad' for Australia, and only 4 percent described themselves as racially 'quite prejudiced'. Yet there is a much larger group expressing less than complete enthusiasm for our cultural mix. Probably the best measure of ethnic and cultural acceptance is a social distance scale. This avoids crude like or dislike questions, instead grading acceptance from 'allow as Australian citizen' through to 'welcome as family', and grading rejection as 'have as visitor only' or 'keep out of Australia'. In a social distance survey done in the late 1980s, Muslims came out as the group least accepted by other Australians. While the absolute social distance scores were highest for Australian-born people, all the major migrant groups concurred that Muslims were the group from which they felt most distant. This is a fault line in Australian society, waiting for an event to turn social distance into something nastier.

Probably the most dangerous event, because it creates the strongest feelings of them and us, is war. We already have an idea of what can happen from the early 1990s, when Australian ships assisted the UN force against Iraq. In a book on the Gulf War, Christine Asmar chronicled some of the difficulties this war created for Arab Australians, who in 1996 numbered about 180,000 (in Australia most Arabs are not Muslim, and most Muslims are not Arab, but the two are often confused). Asmar reports that some Arabs were upset about the war. She quotes a woman of Egyptian origin, the manager of 2EA in Sydney, as saying 'the relentless bombing of Iraq, to me and many Arabs, cannot be seen in terms of defeating one ruler. It is seen in terms of the total destruction of a nation made of people with whom I share a culture ...' Note that this concern is not in the liberal language of concern for a common humanity, but the particularist concern for fellow Arabs and the culture she shares with them. A number of Arab groups, including Lebanese Muslims (Lebanese Christians have been less active in pan-Arab causes) and Palestinians opposed the war. The local representative of the PLO even refused to condemn Iraq's invasion of Kuwait, saying that it 'only serves to block the dialogue that is needed to arrive at a peaceful solution'. Others, however, supported the war, particularly those from Iraq itself, who had experienced Saddam Hussein's regime first hand.

Australian Arabs, whether they opposed the war or not, did suffer verbal and physical harassment during the war. There were reports of Arab children being abused from passing cars and intimidated at school, Muslim Arab women having their head scarves ripped off, mosques receiving bomb threats, and break-ins at Arab community centres. The NSW Anti-Discrimination Board found that Arab Australians were the most vilified of any ethnic group.

Similar stories are again being heard during this conflict. In the days following the September 11 attacks, newspapers reported numerous anti-Muslim incidents. These included stones and bottles being thrown at a bus carrying Muslim children, faeces being thrown into the grounds of a mosque, and hate mail and phone calls. A mosque was subsequently destroyed by fire. Churches were also set alight; whether these were random acts of arson or revenge attacks is not clear.

The political response to these communal tensions was probably better this time than in the early 1990s. NSW Premier Nick Greiner, leader at that time of the State that is home to more Arabs (and Muslims) than any other, was quick to condemn harassment and violence, and to defend the right of Arabs to express their views. Other political leaders, especially Prime Minister Bob Hawke, were slower to issue statements, though he eventually did. This time, political leaders were quickly photographed at mosques. There has been clear, bipartisan signalling that Muslim Australians are part of the Australian community. This is an important part of any strategy to deal with fears people have.

While political support is important, Muslim communities still have a difficult task. The fears some non-Muslim Australians have about the Muslim community could be classed as improbable but not irrational. In both the Gulf War and the current conflict, there are members of the Muslim community who oppose war due to ethnic or religious solidarity with Australia's opponents. There is a fine line between this and supporting forces that could kill Australian troops. That terrorism is a standard tactic of Islamist extremists makes this attitude more concerning, as does the fact that the September 11 hijackers looked 'normal' to Western eyes: they could have wandered the streets of multicultural cities like Sydney or Melbourne without attracting a second look or thought. This means that even an assimilationist strategy will not, to some, be absolutely convincing.

Nevertheless, emphasising Australian loyalties is a critical strategy for Muslim communities. Studies by social psychologists of how to reduce inter-group prejudice find that an important factor is the development of dual identities. People respond much more positively to people they perceive as being part of their own group, with whom they share an identity. The Muslim way of life, with its attitudes toward religious observance, gender roles and much else cannot possibly be the basis of a shared identity with the more numerous secular and Christian Australians. The most practical way to create a common identity is through an over-arching commitment to Australia as a nation.

This strategy is in fact being adopted, to some extent. Christine Asmar says that the term 'Arab-Australian' came into common use during the Gulf War, both as a way of unifying disparate Arab communities in the face of a common threat, and as a way of signalling to other Australians that 'we are Australians first and Arabs second'. In the war on terrorism, Australian Muslims were very quick to act when the media (with some exaggeration, as it turned out) reported that the Taliban Ambassador to Pakistan had announced a *jihad* against Australia. Muslim leaders were quick to say that Australian Muslims should ignore the call.

This action was sensible and timely. Yet the involvement of Muslim groups in the anti-war movement is, from the point of the view of the immediate problems facing Muslim communities in Australia, unfortunate. Whatever the logic of their arguments, they give the impression that they do not share most other Australians' view that strong action is needed against terrorists and those who shelter them. Nothing could better show Muslim loyalty to Australia than a capacity to put aside Muslim solidarity in favour of Australian interests. The symbolism of this would be more powerful than anything else the Muslim community could ever do to ensure their full acceptance into Australian society. It would call the bluff of the Norman Tebitts. This opportunity is not being taken.

Samuel Johnson once remarked that 'patriotism is the last refuge of a scoundrel'. It can also be the last refuge of a liberal. Liberals can easily convince themselves of the merits of a diverse society, and can put in place laws to protect that society. But not everyone is so enamoured of diversity in itself, and it is in the nature of a liberal society that state control is not pervasive, and so laws can only achieve so much. For the people who don't find diversity attractive, you have to invent ways of showing that there are unities that transcend the differences.

Historically, love of country has proven to be a more powerful force than love of liberal principles. Quite possibly we are seeing this in public reaction to the boat people; turning them back is seen as an assertion of Australia's right to control its borders, and this outweighs any claims the boat people may have as members of persecuted groups. Some are quick to denounce what they see as the illiberalism of turning back the boats. But the sentiment underlying the policy's popularity may well be critical to long-term acceptance of Muslim Australians, since they too can show their commitment to Australia. The United States is so aware of this idea that they made the link between diversity, unity, and country their motto: *e pluribus unum*, one out of many. Liberals can use patriotism to pursue their goals, persuading Muslim Australians to confirm their Australian identity, and then encouraging Australian patriots that they do share at least one thing with the Muslim minority.

Towards a New Ethic of Civilisational Discourse

Muqtedar Khan

The war on terrorism is not likely to end quickly. Some elements in Washington expect it to last a generation. As long as the cycle of terror and counter-terror continues, the relations between Islam and the West will remain strained and contentious. Muslims in the West will continue to find themselves in a precarious situation, oscillating between two poles – suspects and cultural bridges. Intellectuals, concerned citizens and political leaders in the West as well as in the Muslim world will have fundamentally to rethink their positions and strategies in order to escape a prolonged cycle of war and terror. Muslim intellectuals in the West will have to realise their potential to become cognitive bridges and advance new paradigms on the basis of which peace activists and cultural and community ambassadors can undermine and subvert the forces of war and terror.

M.A. Muqtedar Khan is Assistant Professor of Political Science and the Director of International Studies at Adrian College, Michigan. He is also the Vice President of the Association of Muslim Social Scientists and is on the board of the Center for the Study of Islam and Democracy.

There are three dangers against which all peace loving people must be on guard:

> This conflict must not be allowed to become a clash of civilisations, between Islam and the West/Rest.
>
> Hawks and extremists must not be allowed to hijack and dominate the discourses in the West and in the Muslim world.
>
> The search for security and revenge should not be allowed to undermine the moral fabric of our societies.

Defend Dissent and Difference in America

Hawks in the West who may entertain Islamophobic sentiments must abstain from exhorting the American government to extend its bombing campaign to other Muslim nations. Indiscriminate bombing will only lead to further anger and hatred against the West and will incite more violence from militant Muslims. Some of these hawks are now claiming 'we are all Israelis'. This implies that, since the US has now also become a victim of political violence of Muslim extremists, it is time the US also responded in the same way as Israel.

Americans must guard against such bad advice from those friends of Israel who are pessimistic about the prospects of peace between Israel and Palestine and would like nothing better than to get the US to do its dirty work, such as eliminating all Palestinian resistance to Israel in the name of fighting terrorism. Heavy-handed military tactics as displayed in Ariel Sharon's present tenure have done little to enhance Israeli security, but have plunged the nation into a never-ending spiral of violence.

America does not wish to enter into a never-ending violence with Muslims, who number over 1.4 billion and live in nearly all nations of the earth. Israeli military tactics have severely undermined its claims to being the only democracy in the Middle East. Surely America does not wish to destroy its own democracy to pursue Israeli interests. Even though the new terrorism bill and the new executive order permitting the use of military tribunals for trials and executions have already jeopardized the Bill of Rights and pushed the US down several notches on the scale of democracy, it should not try to become another Israel.

It is the responsibility of the American media and American intellectuals and peace lovers to ensure that hawks and warmongers do not monopolize the national agenda. So far the American media has not done justice to its role as the voice of the people and the conscience of the government. By completely capitulating to the governmental agenda they have become to the US what *Pravda* used to be to the USSR – state sponsored media.

Loud dissent and systematic criticism of the manner in which the Bush administration is conducting this war on terrorism is absolutely necessary to ensure that excesses at home or abroad are not committed. The war against terror should not itself become terror at home or overseas. The moral responsibility of ensuring this lies with the political opposition, the media, academics and public intellectuals, and commentators. I hope that in the interests of American security and democracy, these voices will speak up and be heard.

Moderate voices in America must defend American democracy and resist the danger that hasty and undebated legislations and executive orders pose to the civil rights of minorities. A paranoid government should not be allowed essentially to rewrite the US constitution. Moderate voices in America must also speak up and challenge the dangerous domination of misguided patriotism before the war on terror becomes a war on dissent and difference in America.

The dominant discourse in America is focusing on two issues − understanding Islam and building national unity. Both these themes are problematic. While there is a lot of positive reflection and discussion of Islam, the heightened interest in Islam inevitably stems from the fundamental assumption that somehow Islam is behind the horrible tragedies of September 11. This is not only a great insult to one of civilisation's greatest traditions, it is also strategically misleading. A better understanding of Islam, however desirable, will not lead to an understanding of why September 11 happened.

Americans may find more answers if they placed their foreign policy under the microscope. It is time they stopped obsessing over bin Laden and Islam and examined the recent history of their actions overseas to grasp the depth of hatred they engender among foreigners. A quick look at the State Department's annual report on terrorism will show that nearly 60 percent of all anti-US terrorist acts happen in Latin America. Neither an absence of democracy or presence of Islam will explain why the democratic and unIslamic Latin Americans hate the US.

In search of unity, American leaders are compromising the most important aspect of American society – freedom. It is time we realize that it is not insecurity but forced unity which is the biggest threat to freedom in America. Since September 11, I have spoken at many universities across the nation, been on tons of radio and TV shows and written for nearly 100 different media outlets. I have noticed a huge difference in what is said in the media and what is said across campuses by professors as well as students. I know this for certain: all Americans' voices are today not represented either in the media or in the government.

Students and academics all across America are not only critical of American foreign policy but also deeply afraid of the deterioration of the protection of civil liberties in America. Most of them wish to revamp old notions of national interest and advocate a more benign international outlook. Many are deeply disturbed by the violence the US itself seems to be capable of. But sadly, many of them are afraid to speak out in public outside university campuses, or in the media. This fear, this insecurity, this loss of freedom is not because of the terrorist attacks of September 11, but because of the attacks on dissent and difference by the government and the media in the aftermath of September 11. It is not the terrorists, but our search for a national unity, that is destroying our freedoms.

Muslims Must Enjoin Moderation and Forbid Extremism

> We made you a nation of moderation and justice
> *(Koran, 2:143)*
> To advocate what is right and forbid what is wrong
> *(Koran, 3:110)*

What happened on September 11 in New York and Washington will forever remain a horrible scar on the history of Islam and humanity. No matter how much we condemn it, and point to the Koran and the Sunna to argue that Islam forbids the killing of innocent people, the fact remains that the perpetrators of this crime against humanity have indicated that their actions are sanctioned by Islamic values.

The fact that even now several Muslim scholars and thousands of Muslims defend the accused is indicative that not all Muslims believe that the attacks are unIslamic. This is truly sad.

Muslim moderates in the West as well as in the Muslim world must become aggressive in their dealings with the extremists in their midst. The first step is to recognise that when moderates remain silent extremists speak for all. Those Muslims who do not wish to be represented by the likes of Osama bin Laden must speak out loud and clear. They must let the world know in no uncertain terms that terrorists like bin Laden do not represent them. What is also extremely crucial is that they reject specific interpretations of Islam and Islamic principles that people like bin Laden use to justify the murder of innocent civilians, women and children.

If they choose to remain silent, for whatever purpose, then they must share the blame for the association of Islam with terrorism. They must also not complain if the rest of the world mistakes their cowardly silence on terrorism as support for terrorism and terrorists. Moderate Muslims must also remember that vague and generalised statements condemning terrorism are not helpful. They must condemn specific acts and specific individuals and groups associated with those acts. If you are against terrorism then let the world know that in unequivocal terms.

Many Muslims, including some American Muslims, have become hypocritical in our advocacy of human rights and in our struggles for justice. We protest against the discriminatory practices of Israel, India, and other non-Muslim nations, but are mostly silent against the discriminatory practices in Muslim states.

The Israeli occupation of Palestine is perhaps central to Muslim grievance against the West. While acknowledging that, I must remind you that Israel allows its one million Arab citizens more political rights and freedom of speech than most Arab nations allow their citizens. We rightly condemn Israeli treatment of Palestinians at all international forums. But our silence at the way many Muslim nations have treated the same Palestinians really questions our commitment and concern for them. Isn't it a tragedy that in spite of all the Muslim support for Palestinians, more Western nations than Muslims nations allow them to become their citizens?

While we loudly and consistently condemn Israel for its ill treatment of Palestinians and Russian excesses in Chechnya or Serbia atrocities in Bosnia, we remain silent when Muslim regimes abuse the rights of Muslims and slaughter thousands of them. Where were we when Saddam used chemical weapons against Muslims (Kurds)? Or when the Pakistani army massacred Muslims (Bengalis)? When Syria massacred thousands of Islamists in Hama, did we launch a campaign against Syria? Have we demanded international intervention or retribution against Muslim nations that commit egregious violations of Muslim human rights? Is our lukewarm criticism of Muslim regimes the Islamic way? Are Muslims not supposed to stand for justice even if it means taking a position against our dear ones? *(Koran, 6:152)*

It is time that we faced these hypocritical practices and struggled to transcend them.

Muslims love to live in the US but also love to hate it. Many openly claim that the US is a terrorist state but they continue to live in it. Their decision to live in the United States is testimony that they would rather live here than anywhere else. As an Indian Muslim, I know for sure that nowhere on earth, including India, will I get the same sense of dignity and respect that I have received in the US. No Muslim country will treat me as well as the US has. If what happened on September 11 had happened in India, the world's largest democracy, thousands of Muslims would have been slaughtered in riots on mere suspicion and there would be another slaughter after confirmation. But in the US, bigotry and xenophobia have been kept in check. In many places hundreds of Americans have gathered around Islamic centres in symbolic gestures of protection and embrace of American Muslims. In many cities Christian congregations have started wearing *hijab* to identify with fellow Muslim women. In patience and in tolerance ordinary Americans have demonstrated their extraordinary virtues.

For decades we have watched as Muslims in the name of Islam have committed violence against other Muslims, from the Iran-Iraq war to the struggles in Afghanistan. As Muslims can we condone such inhuman and senseless waste of life in the name of Islam? The culture of hate and killing is tearing away at the moral fabric of Muslim society. We are more focused on 'the other' and have completely forgotten our duty to Allah. In pursuit of the inferior *jihad* we have sacrificed the superior *jihad*.

Today the century old Islamic revival is in jeopardy because we have allowed insanity to prevail over our better judgment. It is time we put an end to this madness. It is time that Muslim moderates rescued Islam and Muslim causes from the clutches of extremists.

As I see it, the only way out is through an extreme intolerance for intolerance. Moderate Muslims must fight against all forms of prejudice, hatred and intolerance within Muslim ranks and militantly advocate peaceful resolutions of conflict within and without the community. Indeed Muslim moderates must wage war against war and realise the Koranic mandate that Muslims are a nation of moderation and justice. *(Koran, 2:143)*

Privilege Morality over Strategy

There are two levels at which one can respond to any crisis: at the moral level and at the strategic level. Strategic responses are usually designed to prevent future crisis, minimise present damage and also provide an *explanation* of how what happened, happened. Strategic responses are often based on technological premises and guided by the amorality of *realpolitik*. Moral responses on the other hand seek an *understanding* of what happened and deal with the issue from a humanist perspective.

Both the West and the Muslim World have responded to the attacks of September 11 from a strategic perspective. Without really caring for what has motivated such extreme actions against the US, the US and its allies have launched a series of strategic and technical campaigns designed towards diminishing the capacity of potential attackers and their allies. The Muslim world has also responded strategically. Muslim states have moved with incredible haste to safeguard their national interests while Muslim civil society, particularly in the West, has geared up to defend itself as if it were involved in a war between Islam and the west.

The dangers of strategic responses and *realpolitik* thinking are that they marginalise morality; and, in my mind, our morality is our humanity. If we put aside our morality we will indulge in inhuman acts. When strategic discourse becomes dominant, the principle of *reciprocity* becomes the overriding concern. Tit for tat, an eye for an eye, become the order of the day. Terror and counter-terror become a way of life. The recent state of affairs in Palestine and Israel, since October, 2000, is a good example of the degeneration of order and quality of life when strategic thinking consumes everyone.

From an Islamic standpoint, the domination of strategic thinking and the principle of reciprocity are unacceptable. Muslims are supposed to be a moral community whose Islamic mandate is to enjoin good and forbid evil. The objectives of the Islamic way are to establish a just society and an environment that facilitates the perfection of the soul. A strategic environment is detrimental to the moral health of the individual soul as well as the social fabric of the society.

When society is gripped in a strategic struggle and reciprocity becomes the overriding principle, the humanity of the self becomes contingent on the humanity of the other. If we allow our actions and our responses to be dictated by the actions of others, then both self and the other mirror each other. We will remain human only if the other chooses to remain human. It is indeed ironic that we allow our humanity to be dictated by the choices of our enemies.

When the US responds to the murder of innocent people with massive attacks that kill more innocent people, then it is merely responding to terror with terror. When Islamic scholars claim that suicide bombings against Israel are permissible because the Israeli army also kills civilians and children, then they have conceded the interpretation of Islamic law to the Israeli army. Regardless of what 'the other' does, we must be careful to respond by remaining within the boundaries of our own morality.

Strategic thinking is necessary, but not at the cost of our morality and humanity. We must not allow the inhumanity of 'the other' to strip us of our humanity.

The best way to ensure that this war on terror does not escalate is by advancing a new discourse. Unlike the present discourse, whose central themes are Islamic terrorism and Western colonialism, we need to explore themes that talk about bridging the gap between Islamic values and Muslim practices, and democratic values and American foreign policy.

The new discourse will emerge if the moderates within the Muslim world and in the West seriously begin collective exercises in self-reflection and self-criticism to bridge the chasm between values and actions, deeds and words, between ideas and realities.

Scratching Beneath the Surface

Leanne Piggott

In the November, 2001, edition of the London-based *Palestine Times*, Palestinian Islamist journalist, Khalid Amayreh, published an article entitled, 'Why I Hate America'. Here, in a frank and bold statement, he articulated one of the defining sentiments of Islamism which has been widely published in the Arab media, though not often translated and reported in the West. 'I would be dishonest if I said I didn't hate the American government', says Amayreh. 'I do hate it, so really, so deeply and, yes, so rightly. America is the tormentor of my people. It is to me, as a Palestinian, what Nazi Germany was to the Jews. America is the all-powerful devil that spreads oppression and death in my neighbourhood'.

Any historian familiar with the realities of 'what Nazi Germany was to the Jews' would dismiss Amayreh's analogy as an extreme hyperbolic fantasy. Yet Amayreh is not the first to refer to America as the devil. 'The Great Satan'

Leanne Piggott is a lecturer in Modern Middle East Studies in the Department of Government and International Relations at The University of Sydney. Her main area of expertise is the Arab/Israeli conflict. Committed to peace and secuity in the wider Middle East, Leanne is a member of the International Commission for Security and Cooperation in West Asia.

has been a name synonymous with the United States in Islamist circles ever since the Iranian Ayatollah Khomenei popularised it in the late 1970s.

In the eyes of Amayreh, the entire suffering of the Palestinian people specifically, and the Arab world in general, is the fault of the United States: 'America,' he asserts, 'is the author of 53 years of suffering, death, bereavement, occupation, oppression, homelessness and victimisation … the usurper of my people's right to human rights, democracy, civil liberties, development and a dignified life … America is the tyrant, a global dictatorship that robs hundreds of millions of Arabs and Muslims of their right to freely elect their governments and rulers because corporate America dreads the outcome of democracy in the Muslim world …'

It seems that Amayreh's hatred has clouded his judgement. No Arabs or Muslims, except those who live in the West, have at any time in their history enjoyed the full complement of 'human rights, democracy, civil liberties, development and a dignified life'. And far more than America dreads the outcome of democracy in the Arab Muslim world, the Islamic clerics who rule Iran dread the outcome of democracy in their own country. It is hypocritical for Amayreh to bewail the absence of democracy and human rights in the Muslim world as a consequence of American policy. Since time immemorial, such values have either been completely unknown in that part of the world or understood in a very different way.

Amayreh then asks what options he is left with. Only two, he says: 'Either I submissively accept perpetual enslavement and oppression … or become an Osama bin

Laden'. It's not that he wants to hate, explains Amayreh, because 'hate can be blind and deadly. But, I also know that oppression, as the Holy Koran clearly states, is worse than murder. I try to control my hate ... But I know too well that I can't be free from the effect until I am free from the cause, and the cause is America's greed, rapacity and hegemony ... Please, America, don't make me an Osama bin Laden'. And with these words Amayreh absolves himself and Osama bin Laden of any personal responsibility for whatever bestial acts they may choose to commit in response to the real or imagined wrongs of the Great Satan.

Amayreh's sentiments in less crude form have been echoed even by some Muslims living in Western countries. For example, in the December 1, 2001, edition of the *Sydney Morning Herald*'s weekend magazine, *Good Weekend*, in the context of a round table discussion between six Australian Muslims, one Muslim argued that the source of corruption in the Middle East is the West: 'Every single regime that has been secular and progressive in the Arab world has been crushed by Western powers, this is the simple reality. Every single so-called fundamentalist regime in the Arab world, which is almost exclusively the very rich Gulf states, has been completely propped up and supported by the West ... The reason why, for example, so-called fundamentalists are so powerful in the West Bank and in Gaza and in Egypt and elsewhere is because they're actually highlighting the corruption and the hypocrisy of either the Western-backed fundamentalist [states] or the Western-backed secularist [states]'.

The recurring themes of Arabist and Islamist apologists are the abdication of responsibility, blaming America (or the West) for everything, and a seeming inability to face up to the indigenous roots of the oppression, injustices and economic backwardness which presently bedevil the Arab world. True responsibility for the chronic failures of states in the modern Middle East, although affected by Western interests, ultimately lies at the feet of Arab regimes which are as autocratic as the Muslim Caliphates of past centuries.

While it can hardly be denied that America has failed in many of its foreign policy decisions in the Middle East (and elsewhere) it is simplistic, when trying to understand the root cause of September 11, to focus on those failures alone. Indeed, if we take bin Laden at his word, the issues which motivated him and his al-Qaeda network were totally different from what their apologists said they were. In video recordings after the World Trade Centre and Pentagon attacks, bin Laden made it abundantly clear that his immediate motivation was to avenge and put an end to the 'infidels defiling holy Arabia'. Put differently, the presence of American troops in Saudi Arabia is considered by Muslims to be an anathema to Islam. Saudi Arabia is *waqf*, or holy land, due to the fact that it is the location of the two holiest sites of Islam, Mecca and Medina. Bin Laden's long-term motivation was reflected in his mention of 'the humiliation and disgrace' suffered by Islam for 'more than eighty years'. The date chosen makes the point very clear. The Islamists believe that ever since the collapse of the last Muslim Empire, the Ottomans, Islam has suffered defeat and humiliation at the hands of the 'infidels', particularly America.

Based on bin Laden's own statements, therefore, the plight of the Palestinians (of whom he initially made no mention), American support for Israel, the sanctions against Iraq and the propping up of the corrupt oil regimes of the Gulf region were not individually or collectively central to the September 11 attacks. If any of these issues had been a primary motivating factor, they would have been highlighted in the choice of targets just as meticulously as every other aspect of the operation. For the perpetrators, the problem is not simply what America does, but what America *is*. That is why they chose as their targets the symbols of US military and economic power. Symbols of America's secular political power and of its strategic and economic strength had also been the focus of bin Laden's previous attacks on targets such as the US military residence in Dhahran, Saudi Arabia in 1996 and the American embassies in Kenya and Tanzania in 1998.

What, then, is America in the mindset of bin Laden and his followers? It is important at the outset to distinguish between traditional Islamic precepts and the way in which Islamists have interpreted them and used them as a pretext for their political objectives. Islam divides the world into two realms: the *dar al-Islam* (the territory of Islam) where Islam is dominant, and the *dar al-harb* (the territory of war, or enemy territory) where Islam is not dominant – yet. It is the duty of every Muslim to wage *jihad* against the *dar al-harb* until it ceases to exist and the whole world is *dar al-Islam*.

However, Muslims have differed sharply over what *jihad* means. The literal meaning of the word *jihad* is 'striving' or 'effort and exertion'. It has often been translated as 'holy war' and this concept has been used by some Muslims throughout history to justify the expansion of political control into non-Muslim regions. Many traditional Muslim scholars argue that the term *jihad* has been mistranslated and misused. They emphasise the personal application of the term *jihad*, and the need for personal striving to comply with the dictates of Islam. The concept of *jihad* is distinguished from that of *qital* (fighting) particularly with regard to the use of force against other societies.

While the distinction may ring true for many Muslims, who also remind us of the Koranic prohibition against killing, there are some Islamic tenets that do condone the initiation of force by Muslims against non-Muslims. Although some modern Muslim writers claim that *Shari'a* permits the use of force only in self defence, the majority of Islamic jurists acknowledge that both the Koran and *Sunna* (teachings) also sanction the initiation of force in propagating the faith. There is abundant evidence of the predominance of this idea in the early history of Islam. In the latter half of the seventh century, Muslim armies of Arabia moved northward to conquer and rule over the whole of what is today Syria, Iraq, North Africa, Spain, Iran and northern India. The *Sunna* records the Prophet's instruction to Muslim armies as follows:

> If you encounter an enemy from among the non-Muslims, then offer them three alternatives. Whichever of these they may accept, agree to it and withhold yourself from them: So call them to embrace Islam. If they accept, then agree to it and withold yourself from them. If, however, they refuse, them call them to pay the *jizya* [tax]. If they accept, then agree to it and withhold yourself from them. If

they refuse, then seek help from God and fight
them.

If the majority view of Muslim jurists is correct,
namely, that Islam does sanction the initiation of force for
propagating the faith, then it brings *Shari'a* into direct conflict with the principles of modern international law and
the UN Charter. This is so even though controversies still
exist within Islam about the nature and magnitude of the
force that may be used.

Although *Shari'a* sanctions the use of force to propagate Islam, very few Muslims would agree that this justifies
the appalling and indiscriminate carnage of September 11
carried out against thousands of innocent civilians. But
there is undoubtedly an extremist element in the Muslim
world who hailed the atrocity and who continue to support the use of force against America. Why? In the
mindset of bin Laden and his followers, America represents
the international centre of idolatrous materialism and is
thus an affront to Islamic religious principles. In the
fevered minds of bin Laden and his apologists, America is
the root of all evil in the world and is, accordingly, the
principal obstacle to the realisation of the Islamists' objective: to restructure the world's states and societies according
to the fundamentals of Islam as they interpret them. Bin
Laden and the al-Qaeda network have put on the public
record their belief that the Muslim fighters who caused
Soviet forces to withdraw from Afghanistan were also
directly responsible for the collapse of the communist
atheistic Soviet regime. (They have as yet little understanding of how economic forces bring about the

implosion of closed societies of any kind, including Islamic ones.) In the full flush of religious fervour, the extremist supporters of the September 11 attacks are utterly convinced that America is now the only remaining pillar of infidel power in the world and the only obstacle to bringing the whole world within the fold of *dar al-Islam*. They fantasise about destroying what they perceive to be America's economic, cultural and strategic hegemony so as to enable Islam to establish its own world hegemony.

The interplay of religion and politics has a long history in the Muslim mindset. Indeed, from the establishment of the first *umma* (Muslim community) in Medina in the seventh century C.E., there was never a clear distinction between political and religious leadership. Islam held out Muhammad to be a prophet in the old Biblical tradition: he was both political leader and spokesperson for God. The nature of leadership in the Muslim world remained unchanged until the final collapse of the Ottoman Empire following World War I. It is easy to argue that, to date, the Arab Muslim world has not recovered from this loss of imperial structure as well as its imperial status. Nor have many in the Arab world come to terms as yet with the failure to stop the creation of a Jewish state in the heartland of the Arab Muslim world – with Jerusalem, another Islamic holy site, as its capital. It has also been difficult for them to accept the loss of their own territory to Israel in war, and their failed attempts to recapture it. And one of the bitter lessons of the Second Gulf War (1990–1991) was that after one Arab state invaded another, only a Western-led alliance was capable of remedying the aggression.

In addition to their military defeats, the Arab states have been humiliated by their repeated failures at modernising their economies despite the fact that they own the world's largest known reserves of oil. According to the World Bank, the average annual income in the Muslim countries in 2000 was only half the world average. In the realm of politics, too, the record is one of unrelieved failure. European imperial powers had established modern state systems in the Middle East in the first half of the twentieth century, based on Western style parties and parliaments. Almost all have ended in corrupt tyrannies. Once in power, single-party dictatorships are nearly impossible to overthrow.

The litany of failures extends to the lack of respect for basic human and civil rights in Arab states. Saddam Hussein did not hesitate to use chemical and biological weapons against his own citizens, and the late Hafez al-Assad, the President of Syria, massacred between 20,000 and 30,000 Syrian protestors in Hama in 1982. Syria presently occupies Lebanon with approximately 30,000 troops and a sizeable number of *mukabarat* (secret police). And since Yasser Arafat moved to Gaza in the mid-1990s, the human rights record of the Palestinian Authority is as abysmal as that of its Arab and Muslim neighbours. This is a great tragedy due to the high expectations the Palestinian people had of their own leadership after decades of Israeli rule.

The message of September 11 is thus clear. The Arab and Muslim Middle East has failed at modernity. What cuts even deeper into the people's wounds is the knowledge that their failures are juxtaposed with the successes of the West. Islamists, unable to face this unpleasant truth, maintain that modernity has failed. The Islamists' proposed solution: bring down America and Muslims will be able to depose and remove their present un-Islamic rulers. They hoped that America, drawn to Afghanistan in response to the terrorist attacks, would suffer the same fate as the Soviet Union a decade earlier. But whether America had intervened in Afghanistan or not, it would have continued to be the target of extremist violence unless or until, according to the al-Qaeda paradigm, it succumbs to Islamic rule. What is not understood by bin Laden and other Islamists, however, is that by rejecting the core values of modernity which have led to the success of the West, the Islamists' *ipso facto* reject the means by which Arab Muslim societies may begin to compete with the West in any meaningful way.

This is surely not going to be a short term contest. In analysing the crime of September 11, serious acknowledgment and responses must be given to the failed state system in the Arab Muslim world and its indigenous sources. Whilst some might argue that Western-style democracy is the panacea for all ills in the Middle East, such Western centred views are also not helpful. One of the lessons of the 1979 Iranian Revolution is that the introduction of western models and values in the Middle East must be sensitive to indigenous culture and beliefs. Points of intersection must be sought between the Middle East and the West.

More broadly, there is considerable scope for a softening of the way Arab Muslims and Westerners perceive each other. Non-Muslims can acknowledge that many sincere Muslims find modern life in the West to be spiritually arid and profoundly unfulfilling. Muslims, on the other hand, can recognise the need to let go of the illusion that Western prosperity can be enjoyed without substantial concessions to the Western political and economic culture of rights and freedoms. Neither world values either material or spiritual impoverishment. The possibility therefore exists for education to break down cultural barriers and misunderstandings.

The real tragedy of the so-called 'war on terror' lies in the number of innocent people who will die and suffer in its wake. Those who were killed and maimed in the attacks on September 11 were not the captains of American economic and military power. They were ordinary working people including, no doubt, a significant number of Muslim Americans, doing nothing more sinister than earning a living to support themselves and their families. Judging by the fate of all other 'isms' that have presented themselves as a panacea for the ills of the Arab Muslim world over the past century, Islamism too will eventually be revealed to be nothing more than a tool to coerce the masses and establish the power and dictatorship of a small band of men. As the Lebanese academic Fuad Ajami so profoundly concludes in his book, *The Arab Predicament*:

> At the root of the nativist view of the world is a utopia — a memory of a world that once was that can be adorned, worked over, and embellished to suit current needs. In the modern world, utopias can serve as correctives, as antidotes to cynicism, as

sources of inspiration. But utopias can be pushed too far. Our [Arab Muslim] imagined utopias turn out to be the sources of much of our misery: We never quite approximate them, and we feel all the more diminished for failing to replicate the glories of our ancestors or the perfection of our plans.

Modern Civilisation and its Malcontents

Roger Sandall

'Civilisation is Genocide'. This sign at a recent Berlin rally shows what we are up against – people who live in modern cities, who are the beneficiaries of modern civilisation and all it offers, who expect food in the stores and medicine at the chemist's and police to keep order in the streets, and who nonetheless want to tear all this up by the roots. An al-Qaeda caveman in his cave studying flight schedules is one thing. As a mass murderer he's a declared enemy of mankind. But the 'Civilisation is Genocide' crowd and the hare-brained WTO demonstrators are men and women who look superficially like us, are usually citizens like the rest of us, and are perfectly entitled to speak their minds. The problem is that their minds have somehow become horribly twisted – so twisted that they actually appear in favor of the homicidal barbarism which flew those planes into the World Trade Centre; so warped that they are quite possibly clinically deranged.

Roger Sandall *is a former contributor to* Encounter, Commentary, *and* Art International, *and the author of* The Culture Cult: Designer Tribalism and Other Essays *(Westview Press, 2000).*

The paradox is striking. Economically, and in numerous other ways, no civilisation in the past has provided so many benefits to so many ordinary people as ours does today. In the strange case of the US, we see a country unable to stop uninvited guests, coming from all over the globe, pouring across its feeble and ill-defended frontiers – people willing to do literally anything to gatecrash the American party in the hope of improving their lives. Yet has any great civilisation of the past had to deal with quite so many enemies within? So many alienated intellectuals filled with cultural self hate? So many eager to pull their own world down – and violently if need be, too?

Think of it a moment. If somebody actually believes civilisation is genocide, what's he likely to do? Since genocide equals racism equals the supreme evil of the modern age, then presumably anything is justified against it, and civilisation in its entirety is a legitimate target. Treasonous activity likely to weaken or destroy one's homeland becomes virtuous and admirable. Wiping out the institutions of modern life becomes a moral imperative, and flying hijacked civilian airplanes into skyscrapers is just a start. According to the logic of our Berlin protester, both biological and chemical warfare are legitimate and proper forms of assault. Whether a scenario along these lines will indeed unfold remains to be seen: at present 'Civilisation is Genocide' is more a slogan than a movement. But the World Trade Centre bombing and the anthrax attack do not encourage complacency.

What's the matter? Why does our civilisation seemingly inspire more hatred than affection? And has this always been the case with the more advanced and progressive social forms? Before trying to answer this question we need to be clear why modern civilisation is unique, and quite unlike all previous civilisations known to history. Politically, the rest of them were a mix of the theocratic, the aristocratic, and the exclusive. In contrast, our own civilisation is secular, democratic, and inclusive – Popper's Open Society writ large. On the economic side all previous civilisations were mainly agrarian, favoring big landowners with large estates. In contrast modern economies are overwhelmingly urban, commercial, and industrial, made up of entrepreneurs and ordinary working people, and especially favoring anyone having technical, managerial, and political expertise and muscle.

On the surface, multifaceted modern civilisation is immediately more attractive than its hierarchic predecessors. So why is it that the numerous advantageous developments it has ushered in drive some of its most conspicuous beneficiaries wild with rage? Why is it that others – mainly outsiders in less favored and more backward lands – want to destroy it outright?

We must first distinguish between modern civilisation's internal and external enemies, for the same things do not necessarily enrage both, or enrage both equally. As regards the causes of internal hostility, and the domestic groups who are disaffected, three problem areas suggest themselves: the unwelcome implications of an Open Society, the psychological pressures of modernisation, and the dismaying consequences of a democratic social order in which the values of the common man (and the common consumer) become an ultimate legitimation. Karl Popper's Open Society sounds like a good thing. How could something so liberal, pluralistic, and humane not be welcome? But the ambiguity of the word 'open' is a warning, and also a clue to what people find so troubling about the direction of modern life. For some men and women openness itself is downright threatening, and the fact must be faced that this undeniable social virtue goes profoundly against humanity's mental grain. Historically, traditionally, tribally, for ages past, what has been *closed* has been synonymous with what was secure and definite and predictable; societies were fortresses in a world of ubiquitous war; while whatever was open was seen as vulnerable, unclear, and unpredictable, in addition to being exposed to every kind of contingent threat.

Who wants to live in a house with a permanently open door? It should be open to some, of course − but come one, come all? Who wants to live in a country with porous or fragile borders? Frontiers that can be invaded by anyone with enough determination, desperation, or gall? Both exclusiveness and the power to exclude make biological, social, and political sense − and there is nothing strange or obscure about this. Exclusiveness and the power to exclude have obvious survival value. On the other hand a quick and short-term view of Popper's ideal society makes it seem as if openness has no such value − indeed, is a downright liability. Restriction and control appear altogether more natural and right. It is obvious that without restriction and control anyone at all might freely enter one's homeland, including the murderous and the deranged.

Which of course they have already done recently in America, and may very well do again. There is nothing whatever paranoid about this assertion. It is firmly based on the self-declared intransigence of the enemy and a calculation of what that enemy may do. Nor do we need to labour the point or moralise about it: the weakness and vulnerability of the Open Society of the US, when exposed to violent undesirables who make their way unchecked across its frontiers, has been dramatised in the most terrible way.

The same tropism that brings the benign and ambitious to America also brings the malign and the vicious too: for some mysterious reason they just won't stay home. Thus Sheik Omar Abdul Rahman, now in jail for bombing the World Trade Centre in 1993, could not and would not remain quietly in Egypt where he lived before. Instead, both he and his accomplice Mahmud Abouhalima (another Egyptian named 'Mahmud the Red' for his red hair), moved from the Middle East to New York, where they settled in, made themselves comfortable, and then did everything they could to destroy their adopted home. Their first effort failed. Yet eventually other fanatical haters with the same ambition levelled the Twin Towers according to plan.

But this takes us away from our true topic at this stage, which is the reason why the Open Society has so many *internal* enemies – not why it attracts enemies in from the outside. And to begin with we have to recognise that openness is an ambiguous virtue, just as freedom is an ambiguous virtue. They are indeed two aspects of the same thing. Both openness and freedom involve risk; and both require a spirit of optimism and trust if the opportunities they present are to be seized. But in addition to this there is something else too. By its very boundlessness and seeming lack of direction the Open Society induces a kind of vertigo which afflicts even its most devoted admirers. So little is known for sure about the future. So little is remembered from the past. Nothing is sacred; time-honoured authority dissolves; all that is solid melts into air.

As a result, the intrinsic uncertainties of the Open Society generate disquiet among many, deep discontent among some, and homicidal fury in a few – and not all of them are Islamic fundamentalists either. In isolated mountain huts potential Unabombers scratch their beards, pore over well-fingered anti-industrial texts, and darkly meditate who and where to strike next.

At the root of all this is a feature of every genuinely Open Society today – the continuous process of modernisation and creative innovation. Upheaval. Destruction. Displacement. Renewal. All of which means here today and gone tomorrow in both the material and the immaterial worlds. And this produces just as much dizziness and resentment and dismay as openness itself. Many people today both on the left and the right fear that things are running 'out of control', fear being left behind and increasingly out of touch, fear that what is most out of control is the pace of change. This fear is entirely understandable. But it is not a helpful response. Without wishing to embrace historical inevitability, or a vision of life as fate, one has to say that the leading edge of civilisation is likely to become less and less subject to conscious human control as time goes by.

The global village is not like Little Puddlington on the Marsh. Nor is it like some medieval mullah-ridden corner of Afghanistan. And it is certainly not like an old-time Aboriginal camp. Where each of these social environments was static and predictable, with established hierarchies of knowledge, status, and power, the world we live in is one of continuously shifting means and ends and personnel. This is deeply disturbing to the kind of mind which expects fixed and universally accepted ends, which admires a stable social order, and which regards both as synonymous with the Good Society. And it is disturbing enough to guarantee the alienation of the political right from modernity, and to generate a deep current of conservative discontent.

Precisely because large parts of our environment are spontaneous, dynamic, and evolving without central direction (can anyone keep track of all the specialised magazines in today's newsagencies, or the niche markets they cater to?) modern industrial and commercial civilisation contains a myriad systems and subsystems entirely beyond our mental reach. The scientific world ramifies infinitely into branches which then themselves divide, and the technological world likewise. Unregulated economic activity continually throws off niche enterprises which grow and split and then create more niches for other firms, fertilised and stimulated by scientific and technological innovation. E-paper – electronically re-usable paper without ink – has been nothing but an idea in an inventor's head for fifteen years: by 2010 it could be a major industry. That is what modern civilisation is like: division, specialisation, ramification, innovation, without end. No-one is in charge. And no single mind can master all of the facts.

The left regards this with even more horror than the

right. It calls for controls, managers, monitors, technocrats, *dirigisme* at any price. This too is an unhelpful and self-defeating reaction. 'The more civilised we become', wrote Hayek, 'the more relatively ignorant must each individual be of the facts on which civilisation depends'. This specialisation has many more benefits than costs – providing free association driven by private interest allows and encourages all the social bits and pieces to join together, and work together, for the common good. Things may very well be out of control, but in Hayek's view they probably should be. He argues that mankind's greatest successes in the past owe much to the fact that we weren't always able to control social life, going on to warn that our 'continued advance may well depend on deliberately refraining from exercising controls which are now within our power'.

But what about the endless creation of the new? This is an aspect of modernity that conservatives and radicals alike find repellent. This is the feature of commercial civilisation they find most offensive and otiose. But the liberal view of innovation is more optimistic, and quite possibly a lot more profound with regard to human nature. In *The Future and Its Enemies*, Virginia Postrel argues that 'the psychological need for novelty is a fundamental characteristic of the human species'. According to her it isn't just faddism, or the artifice of fashion, or the economic need for built-in obsolescence, or a lust for the new just for the sake of the new. Novelty is an essential part of our self-created milieu of constant change, and in this artificial milieu (the artificial environment which anthropologists call 'culture') an alert interest in the new helps human adaptation.

To curb or reject this tendency is undesirable: it would lead to our being less and less able to act adaptively, and to being swept back steadily into the past. That is of course the universal condition of many backward tribal cultures today. The taste for novelty expresses a deeply human capacity and enjoyment – the ability to create and manage a dynamically evolving environment filled with changing elements, personnel, scenarios, and goals. This is the modern environment in which we continually make and remake our social selves.

Civilisation today is not only open, and continuously modernising, it is democratic. So is it democracy perhaps which is unloved? Maybe it is, for since the time of the ancient Greeks it has never had a very good press. We are told that the word 'democracy' was often used by its aristocratic critics in Greece as a kind of epithet, to show their disdain for the common people (or *demos*) who had replaced the aristocratic control of government with their own. For centuries, elites of one sort or another have fought the democratic principle that government should rest on the consent of the governed. And in our own time Winston Churchill was famous for his dryly grudging praise of democracy as the worst possible form of government – 'except for the others'.

Yet democracy is not only an important feature of modern civilisation, it is so important that in many ways the two things are interdependent, if not synonymous. Robert Dahl compiled a list of ten benefits which democracy bestows, and here are four of them. In each case they point to the benefits of modern civilisation too:

- Democracy helps to prevent government by cruel and vicious autocrats.
- Democracy helps people to protect their own fundamental interests.
- Only a democratic government can provide a maximum opportunity for exercising moral responsibility.
- Only a democratic government can foster a relatively high degree of political equality.

Translating these propositions into the terms of our present discussion, let us see how closely modern civilisation and democracy are linked. Modern civilisation helps to prevent the rise of cruel and vicious autocrats because the pluralistic social and economic base of an open society is radically incompatible with one-party, one-boss rule. This could be seen in Soviet Russia, and it can be seen again in Syria and Iraq today – all of them variations on the old theme of Asiatic Despotism. Again, modern civilisation helps people to protect their interests because it insists that the role of individuals, as free social and economic agents, receives equal importance with the claims of community and nation. Where independent citizens are not even allowed to exist, as under the barbaric regime of North Korea, individuals are unable to protect their interests, and thousands are now starving to death.

Similar considerations apply to the remaining items. The absence of individual moral responsibility under despotic regimes is yet another feature decisively setting them off from modernity. So grave are the moral problems of Russia in the aftermath of the Soviet system – the lack of respect for truth, and for everything that inspires trust between one man and another, or between citizens and the state – that it remains to be seen when and if the country will ever recover. As for equality, modern market systems differentially reward different people with different abilities: but at least they try to equalise opportunity at the outset, before the sorting process begins, while a universal franchise guarantees that even those who fail economically are still able to be represented and to have a political voice.

Yet democracy also generates deep currents of discontent today, almost as deep as among the classical thinkers of long ago who saw it as low, degraded, and driven by the passions and appetites of the masses. Intellectual elites across the entire political spectrum find Jerry Springer and his ilk revolting; the sex and violence in mass entertainment irresistibly reminds them of Roman decadence; and the tastes of consumer society seem an unpersuasive substitute for the cultivated tastes of the literate elites of yesterday. A yearning for *dirigisme* on the left, and for aristocracy among at least some people on the right, produces a barely disguised disdain for modern civilisation and a decidedly grudging endorsement of its character and aims.

Against this modern world of change and dynamic variability stands the paralysis and fixity of the old traditional world, a world where the rule that was followed yesterday is the rule that must be followed tomorrow, and tomorrow, and tomorrow, 'to the last syllable of recorded time'. Incredibly, that is the sort of paralysis which Islamic fundamentalism now seeks to impose upon a large part of mankind. What the Koran says is true is said to be true eternally, and the timeless archetype of Islam in the seventh century, the culture of a bunch of desert nomads, becomes a model for the year 2001.

Whereas modern industrial civilisation is open, inclusive, adaptive, protean, and pragmatic, the tribal world is by contrast closed, exclusive, and increasingly maladaptive, its cognitive understandings enshrined by dogma, its inhabitants caught in cultural traps. Where modernity is inclined to say that cultural differences don't matter, the tribal world not only says that cultural differences matter, but that they are all-important − that the identities they mandatorily inscribe and implant are the very essence of life itself. This reactionary response to the modern world is deeply maladaptive, and can only threaten the survival of tribal peoples themselves. When we look at America for comparison, the paradigm of modern civilisation as a polity, we see a nation which has survived all challenges hitherto by *including* a variety of ideas and talents from many places. The value of this policy was shown in World War II. By welcoming what Einstein, Fermi, and Szilard had to offer, it was able to achieve military preponderance when it counted most. As a result modern civilisation came through its worst ordeal.

The clash between these two principles − the inclusive and the exclusive; the open and the closed; the willingness to live in a changing and developing world rather than one which is unchanging and already 'known' in advance − is what underlies the present global convulsion. It had been assumed that the process of economic and political inclusion (or globalisation) would continue more or less unimpeded to the benefit of all concerned. And in many places this has happened. But nobody foresaw the resistance that would be mounted by affronted Arab tribalism — backward, humiliated, resentful, and bent on revenge — when reinforced and disciplined by the pan-tribal religion of Islam.

It is wrong to see the present conflict as a clash of 'civilisations'. It is not. It is a clash between modern universal civilisation and the anachronistic residue of a world that has not kept up. Just as the ex-colonial world has 'failed states' that have never successfully adapted and assimilated the institutions of modernity, so Islam is a 'failed civilisation' that has never successfully crossed into the world of modern political and economic organization. It is well known that much of the Islamic world has still not effectively separated church and state, while Islamic fundamentalism aggressively imposes theocracy when and where it can. But the political failure of Islam to adapt to modernity is much more comprehensive than this. The late Elie Kedourie did us all a favor when, in his book *Democracy and Arab Political Culture*, he set down a list of political features we in the West all take for granted, but that are entirely foreign to the Arab political tradition:

> The notion of a state as a specific territorial entity which is endowed with sovereignty; the notion of popular sovereignty as the foundation of govern-mental legitimacy; the idea of representation, of elections, of popular suffrage, of political institutions being regulated by laws laid down by a parliamen-tary assembly; of these laws being guarded and upheld by an independent judiciary; the ideas of

the secularity of the state, of society being com-
posed of a multitude of self-activating, autonomous
groups and associations – all these are profoundly
alien to the Muslim political tradition.

For one hundred years the opportunity for political
reform and progress has existed. But aside from Turkey the
Islamic peoples of the Middle East have never made that
move. What we see in the ideology of Islamism are little
more than the values of tribal culture writ large. These
favour the defensive, the parochial, the aggressive, the
chauvinistic, and the fearful – not to mention the downright paranoid – along with the diffuse and multivariate
ignorance all these reflect. Tribalism cries 'solidarity forever' as it goes to war, and the solidarity of the Islamic
umma, or worldwide religious community, unites and for-
tifies Islamism too.

Civilised men and women have turned their backs on
this primitive value. In social life they have developed a
taste for the pragmatic and the conciliatory; in law and science they cultivate a respect for truth independent of
religious dogma. They have no war cry, and little taste for
war. Here too of course there are dangers. For the outcome
of the present struggle will depend in large part on
whether a military will exists in the secular, pluralistic, and
pleasure-loving societies of the West, equal to the military
will of old-time Eastern fanaticism where suffering, priva-
tion, and death in religious war, is not only honorable, but
is a route to the hereafter, and guarantees entry to paradise
itself.

The Enlightenment Battles of September 11

Michael Warby

The range of public reactions within the Western intelligentsia to the events of September 11 and their aftermath are made more explicable if they are examined in the context of an ongoing clash between differing Enlightenment traditions.

With the onset of that change in outlook we call the Enlightenment, Western civilisation became marked by the self-conscious application of reason to the transformation of human society and knowledge. While the Enlightenment project arose out of already existing trends, under its influence the West became a civilisation ever more clearly distinguished and transfigured by institutionalised innovation – the process of unending change that we call 'modernisation'.

Apart from the Jacobin phase of the French Revolution, and a few limited episodes, by far the most important

Michael Warby has worked in the public service and in private sector think tanks. He has written on a wide range of issues for newspapers, journals and book collections. He is the author of Past Wrongs, Future Rights *(Tasman Institute, 1997) and* Ellis Unpulped *(Duffy & Snellgrove, 2001).*

of which was the Paris Commune of 1870-71, the 'long' nineteenth century from 1789 to 1914 revealed few of the dark sides of the Enlightenment. These sprang forth in the carnage of World War I – which destroyed overblown expectations of untroubled progress – and the megacidal Enlightenment civil war that framed and marked the 'short' twentieth century of 1914 to 1991: a struggle between adherents of the sceptical Enlightenment vision, of a society of ordered liberty taking human nature largely as a given, and the adherents of the radical Enlightenment vision, of harmony through a purified society and trans- formed humanity. The former was a vision confident in the range of human reason, the latter one intoxicated by it.

This conflict was fought within nations but also between them, as particular states were dominated (or even captured) by one vision or the other. The key states in the sceptical Enlightenment corner were those of Anglo- America. In the radical Enlightenment corner were the Leninist states, beginning with the Bolshevik seizure of power in Russia in 1917, and ending with the evaporation of the Soviet Empire in 1989-91, together with the aban- donment of socialism as a path of modernisation by nearly all the remaining Leninist states. Leninist socialism had proved to be a path to institutionalised innovation in little except the techniques of repression and mass murder.

The collapse of Leninism as a serious transforma- tional project (as distinct from an excuse to hold onto power) has not meant the disappearance of the radical Enlightenment vision, nor the cessation of the Enlighten- ment civil war. On the contrary, it has transmuted into new forms – most obviously, the culture wars of the intelligentsia, especially over the project of creating social harmony through control of language and de-legitimisation of dissenting opinion.

And then September 11

The immediate reaction of much of the Western intelligentsia to the events of September 11 was to continue to fight the familiar culture wars. There were those who interpreted the events with the familiar tropes of anti-Americanism, and those who responded by saying how wicked it was in such circumstances to talk about the wickedness of America: the heirs to the radical Enlightenment in the familiar red corner, those of the sceptical Enlightenment in the blue corner.

But, as the days passed, a shift was notable. Many who might have been expected to have been in the red corner failed to appear there, and some even popped up over on the blue side. Some who started in the red corner shifted ground. More to the point, those who had previously been able to 'set the pace' in moral fashion rapidly found themselves isolated, even defensive. Something was going on.

For the Enlightenment civil war is not a matter of left and right. Rather, the key division is within the left. Equality is the unifying value of the left: the more completely one is committed to it (including in what one is prepared to do to achieve it), the more left one is. But equality as the manifestation of some perfect social harmony is very different from equality as a matter of human dignity and respect. The former rejects the inevitable inequalities of a society of ordered liberty, while the latter seeks to push such societies further in the direction of equality. With the collapse of socialism, the radical Enlightenment vision of equality has been evolving into new forms – notably, identity politics. September 11 was one of those events that made clear, as had the Nazi-Soviet pact and the Berlin blockade, which side of the Enlightenment divide you were really on.

The way the Western culture-war battlelines became re-aligned can be simply expressed. The division is between those who look at the Islamic extremists (implicitly or explicitly) on the basis of 'the enemy of my enemy is my friend', and those who say 'the enemy of both is the enemy of all'. It is between those who take the actual aims of the Islamic extremists seriously, and those who interpret them in terms convenient for further prosecution of the Enlightenment civil war. The 'enemy of my enemy' approach was also pursued by various Christian fundamentalists (who saw the events as the wages of sin), libertarians (who saw them as the wages of overweening government), racist fringe-dwellers (who saw them as the wages of impurity) and anti-globalists (who saw them as the wages of globalisation).

An obvious feature of those who did the deeds of September 11 was that they were not of either faction of the Western Enlightenment. In fact, they hated what the Western Enlightenment represented and had become. This hatred was explicable, since, for many in the Middle East, modernity has been experienced as an imposition, a threat, an assault. Worse, it has been experienced through pastiche imitation, not the thing itself – all the downsides, with few of the benefits.

Everything old becomes new again

But we have been here before. The West has already faced a violent and murderous enemy of both sides of the Enlightenment civil war in military conflict, a military conflict in which an enemy of the sceptical Enlightenment was first effectively supported, and then opposed, by partisans of the radical Enlightenment.

For Western society has not been made up only of the various heirs of the Enlightenment. There is also the counter-Enlightenment: those who have been repelled by the entire Enlightenment project and its consequences. This wave of thought and sentiment brought forward the greatest revolutionary of the twentieth century, the man whose career is the pivot around which that century turns: Adolf Hitler. His Nazi Party was a curious, but effective, amalgam of counter-Enlightenment notions, along with a racial form of the radical Enlightenment purifying project. Like the Leninists, Hitler sought to transform humanity, but on a race rather than on a class basis. Unlike the Leninists, he made no obeisance whatsoever to the forms of democracy, and he explicitly rejected the universalism which has been a hallmark of the Enlightenment.

There are, to be sure, some obvious differences between the Nazis and the Islamic extremists. The Nazis were not overtly religious, though occultism was very much of the Nazi mix. Islam is most certainly a universalist belief, which Nazism simply wasn't. But there are a lot of eerie similarities, which remind us that there is much in the politics of Islamic extremism that has very little to do with Islam. Some similarities are perfectly obvious, such as killing homosexuals, wanting to live in a region without

Jews, and belief in strict gender roles. Others appear on reflection. Both Hitler and bin Laden have traded on the mystique and cameraderie of being war veterans. Both despised Christianity, though Hitler's wish to de-Christianise German society came up against entrenched social realities that he found it expedient not to push too far.

Then there are the similarities of context. Hitler brought the politics of the scapegoat to a peak of efficiency never before equalled. Such politics of hate and paranoia are now common in the Middle East, where scapegoating Israel, the Jews, and the West provides cover for the failures of Arab politics and institutions – so much so, that some mainstream Arab newspapers carried stories seriously seeking to blame the September 11 events on a Jewish conspiracy. While the utility of Israel as hate object for many Arab regimes must lead us to doubt whether a stable peace is likely, achievement of such a peace could lead to even greater turmoil in the region, as such regimes became naked to their failures.

The Germany in which Hitler rose to power was a country with a profound sense of history having gone wrong, rife with territorial grievances and concerns about cultural pollution. All this also exists in the Middle East, especially as Islam is easily interpreted as some sort of promise from Allah that the House of Belief (and particularly the Arabs as witnesses to the original Revelation) should be the centre of the human universe. That profound sense of wrongness fuels so much, as historian Bernard Lewis has explained. All in all, it is not so surprising that Hitler's synthesis of socialism and nationalism has already had plenty of imitators in the region: Qadaffi in

Libya, Assad the elder in Syria, Nasser in Egypt, Saddam Hussein in Iraq. Even in this, imitation has been problematic — nationalism's being a pan-Arab aspiration has bedevilled these separate attempts to find a secular path to modernisation. (And the failure of radical secularism is part of the explanation for the current wave of radical Islamism.) By contrast, appealing to Turkish nationalism was a simpler exercise for Ataturk and his heirs. (The evolution of quasi-Parliamentary regimes in Jordan and Iran, along with the apparent strengthening of Turkish democracy, are signs of hope that a better future is possible in the region.)

The old dance or new steps?

As for the reactions of Western intellectuals to September 11 as repeat performance, in the pro-Western left corner was Orwell's admirer (and forthcoming biographer) Christopher Hitchens, who seemed to need nothing to guide him but his own commitment to truth and willingness to buck fashion. Among those who joined him was writer Salman Rushdie, who had had his own experience of the West as refuge from murderous Islamic obscurantism, along with *The New Republic*, a journal whose commitment to the creation of a better public culture includes a cold-eyed concern for truth and consequences.

In the fellow-traveller corner was a host of people, such as Susan Sontag, Noam Chomsky, John Pilger and many writers in the *Guardian*, *New Statesmen* and *Independent*, and local luminaries such as Morag Fraser (editor of *Eureka Street*) in the *Age* and Guy Rundle (editor of *Arena*) and David Bowman (former editor of the *Sydney Morning*

Herald) in the *Adelaide Review*, all explaining how terribly understandable anti-Americanism was, and displaying lots of it themselves. The *Australian* reported that a Triple-J presenter put up a poster in the ABC's Darwin offices quoting bin Laden: 'There is no place in heaven for imperialist Yankee swine'. The BBC was forced to apologise after a panel discussion on the September 11 atrocity included displays of venomous anti-Americanism, which led to a storm of public protest. To many, the fiery destruction visited on the symbols of American capitalism (the World Trade Centre) and militarism (the Pentagon) must have come as near-perfect masturbatory ideological fantasies. The epitome of all this was the September 18 *Guardian* piece by Charlotte Raven headlined, 'A bully with a bloody nose is still a bully' – a perfect expression of trivialising moral bankruptcy and 'the enemy of my enemy' approach. But it is hard to go past the Somali feminist Hibaaq Osman who, having called for the military overthrow of the Taliban before the UN in 2000, now announced she was against the war: it would appear that anti-Americanism trumps all, including feminism. Andrew Sullivan had great fun on his website paralleling Orwell's diary entries about the defeatism of Western intellectuals during the war against the Nazis with contemporary commentary about the war against the Taliban and al-Qaeda.

It is a standard accusation among much of the Western intelligentsia that the US ignores lots of crimes. Yet those so ready with such accusations typically do exactly the same thing themselves. After all, if the Western intelligentsia was moved merely by scale of death and oppression, anti-communism would be *de rigueur* amongst the intelligentsia, and the Assad regime in Syria, or the Islamist regime in Sudan, or even the Taliban itself, would have copped far more denunciations than Israel. The US at least had the excuse of having to deal with the realities of power politics (and that its government's prime obligation is to its own citizens). The only democracies in the Middle East are the non-Arab states, and staunch Western allies, Israel and Turkey. With the partial exception of the quasi-parliamentary regimes of Jordan and Iran, all the other Middle Eastern states are corrupt tyrannies. Given the importance of oil, policy makers often have little choice about whether to support corrupt tyrannies: the question is more which ones to support. The betrayal by some of the Western intelligentsia of their obligation to truth is motivated by things far more trivial – being seen to be virtuous in the approved form, not being awkward at dinner parties – and so is all the more reprehensible.

Hypocrisy among this group turned up elsewhere too. There was much moaning about the threat to freedom from patriotic fervour, and from criticism of what some intellectuals had said. Charles H. Fairbanks would have a different perspective, having been sacked (and then unsacked, when the case was publicised) as Director of the Central Asian-Caucasus Institute at Johns Hopkins University, for being so incautious as to make the passing remark, 'I'll bet anyone here a Koran on that', at an academic conference discussing September 11. The fuss made about the 'insensitivity' of the remark, and even a grovelling public apology (or should we call that 'self-criticism'?) were not enough to save Fairbanks, though the negative publicity was. In publicising the Fairbanks case, the *New*

Republic editor Peter Beinart also drew attention to other cases: a professor at Orange Coast College in Costa Mesa, California, was indefinitely suspended for offending students with a series of confrontational questions about why Muslims condemn the World Trade Centre attacks but don't condemn terrorism against Israel; a Penn State professor received an e-mail from a top administrator warning him that Iranian and Afghan students would find 'insensitive' his comment that it was worth killing innocents in order to topple the governments of Afghanistan and Iran; and officers of the Berkeley Student Senate proposed raising the school newspaper's rent because it ran a cartoon that depicted two Arabs wearing turbans – with a flight manual in the background – on their way to hell. All these incidents displayed both the humourlessness and the totalitarian mentality of the academic speech police.

Meanwhile, both the BBC and Reuters decided that 'terrorist' was not to be used about the actions of September 11, because it might offend some listeners. Yet what was the purpose of flying civilian airliners packed with hundreds of civilians into skyscrapers full of thousands of civilians if it was not to strike terror? This manifestation of moral nihilism masquerading as linguistic sensitivity was the sort of action which made eminently understandable the majority disapproval ratings for the US news media found in polling. And the media presumably did not help its public standing when its defeatism about the Afghan 'quagmire' speedily proved to be greatly overblown. But such nihilistic linguistic sensitivity, where the feelings of a non-Western fringe counted far more than the families of mostly Western victims, along with defeatism, displayed how deeply imbued 'writing down the West' has become.

Awkwardness about examining what the Islamic extremists really represented was another familiar pattern. It is standard for the treatment of non-Western religions to be vastly different from that meted out to, say, Catholicism. Contrast any of the fashionable panegyrics on Aboriginal spirituality with, for example, the campaign run through the *Sydney Morning Herald* objecting to the fact that the new Catholic Archbishop of Sydney was (gasp!) an orthodox Catholic (a campaign whose answer to the rhetorical question 'is the Pope Catholic?' was apparently 'preferably not').

Of course, most Aborigines are not devotees of traditional Aboriginal spirituality, professing Christianity at a higher rate than the general Australian population. But, since the point is to fight internal Western cultural wars, the actual choices, aims and preferences of the mascots of the moment are beside the point. This attitude could be neatly applied to examining (or, rather, not examining) the aims and objectives of the Islamic extremists. Similarly, while one would normally say that it is unfair to judge a religion by its fanatics, Pamela Bone chose to judge a (Western) religion by someone else's fanatics, as she exploited the fanaticism of September 11 to argue in the *Age* that religious schools in Australia should not receive public funding.

The depths revealed
But all this goes deep into the radical Enlightenment project. The project entails a huge gulf between the activists of the redemptive vision of harmony, and those being

harmonised and redeemed: Leninist regimes were forever claiming to be operating on behalf of the proletariat, even as they ruthlessly suppressed any signs of independent action by said proletariat. The symbol of the proletariat was far more important than the wishes of actual proletarians. In the case of September 11, the same game was played in reverse – the symbol of righteous Muslim anger against the West was much more useful than the unfortunate conclusions that might be drawn from examining the actual aims of the Islamic extremists. As Edward Rothstein pointed out in the *New York Times*, the theory of the 'root causes' of terror is only applied when one sympathizes with its conclusions. (Tony Parkinson robustly made a similar point in the *Age*.) That the American-led intervention in Afghanistan turned out to be a deeply liberating experience was even more awkward for the mindset Rothstein and Parkinson criticised.

But where you are coming from drives how you view events. The sceptical Enlightenment's belief that history reveals people as they are leads to a natural concern with historical causes and a willingness to settle for the awkward compromises of reality. By contrast, the radical Enlightenment's view of history as something to be surpassed, and human nature as malleable, naturally leads to looking at history as a record of unending crimes, resulting from its failure to achieve their standards of perfection. It leads, too, to an indifference towards any serious examination of consequences and likelihoods, since past and present are all just the consequences of oldthink. Thus, when Michael Jacobs, General Secretary of the Fabian society, wrote in the *Observer* that 'To "oppose" globalisation is to deny people

in poorer countries the benefits of knowledge, technological advance, cultural diversity, travel and international
contact which we in the rich world enjoy', he showed a
recalcitrant concern with practical realities rather than
transcendent ambitions:

> There is a genuine anti-globalisation position: it is
> held by Islamic and other religious fundamentalists
> who want to turn back the tide of modernity. But
> no-one in progressive politics should be on their
> side.

Adherence to the radical Enlightenment project
requires defining oneself against the West: otherwise, why
is the project justified? Claims of moral superiority also
require one to define oneself against the mass of society –
and what could be more elevating than a project of moral
perfection? So do the project and status-claims each support the other. Yet, the reality is that the overweening
hubris of the radical Enlightenment project is demonstrably pernicious. In power it creates tyranny and mass
murder; out of power it corrupts journalism, scholarship
and pedagogy.

It is because they define themselves as virtuous,
against fellow Westerners, that the heirs to the radical
Enlightenment react to events in the way they do. To the
extent the Western left succumbs to the temptation to
define itself against the West – a West that embodies its
values far more than any other civilisation does or will – it
will continue to be wrong-footed by events. What the
incinerations of September 11 did was to bring home to

many in the Western left, such as Michael Jacobs, how *Western* they truly are, and how hostile to their values much of the outside world is. Other examples in Britain included *Guardian* commentator Hugo Young, calling for explicit society-wide commitment to basic British civic values, and multiculturalist academic Bikhu Parekh (who had previously described Britishness as 'racially coded') calling for British citizenship ceremonies.

September 11 and its aftermath may be blows from which cultural relativism, and the sentimentalising of non-Western cultures, never recover, with the pictures of liberated Afghani women throwing away their *burqas*, and liberated Afghani men shaving their beards, providing satisfactorily non-Western images to ease the relativists' change of heart. Relativist sentimentalising will, hopefully, no longer be a requirement for being seen as a person of conspicuous compassion. The disaster of Leninism had already revealed what a mirage the radical Enlightenment vision of harmony and social perfection is; now its distortions of understanding and judgement have been exposed again.

But the radical Enlightenment project will go on. It will just transmute, again, into new forms. After all, visions of transformational environmental harmony, another marriage of the counter-Enlightenment with the radical Enlightenment, are already walking among us. The project is too grand and glittering a vision of epoch-making self-importance not to live on. The people of the book are correct: pride is indeed the first sin.

The Allures and Illusions of Politics

Gregory Melleuish

The great paradox of our modern commercial civilisation is that it delivers comfort, security and a sense of ease and yet it is regarded so suspiciously by many of those who enjoy its benefits. Why should this be so? Is it unease with the secularism that underpins so much of modern society? In the modern West the state is not a great and sacred thing embodying some all-encompassing vision, but little more than a contrivance that allows people to live together in relative peace and harmony.

Among the discontented of our world, most of whom derive from the intellectual class, two beliefs are held as a matter of faith. The first is an almost sacred conception of politics as an ennobling enterprise through which individuals fulfil themselves. The second is a faith that redemption can be attained in the here and now through politics. One of the consequences of this faith has been the growing 'politicisation' of all the activities that constitute our life, so that they come to be understood in political terms.

This desire to make everything political, and therefore both contentious and capable of being resolved through political means, is at odds with what, I believe, is unique about Western civilisation. This is the view, mentioned above, that politics is a secular activity, one that does not possess special qualities. It also involves a recognition that politics can be a harsh and unsavoury business but one in which people must participate if even greater evil is not to occur.

The events of September 11 and its aftermath reinforce this core belief of Western civilisation. Both the terrorist acts of bin Laden and the responses of those who blamed America for his actions were premised on a political view of the world that put far more faith in politics as a means of transforming the world than they deserve.

These events have drawn me back to consider the dawn of Western civilisation and the key figure in the birth of the intellectual tradition that defines that civilisation: Augustine of Hippo. In the works of Augustine can be found the genesis of that outlook on the world that separates out the religious and the political enterprises, an outlook that defines and distinguishes the West. Yet in the world of late antiquity the path pointed out by Augustine for the Latin West was not the only one possible: other heirs of the Graeco-Roman world, including the Greek Orthodox tradition, the Monophysite and Nestorian Christians and, of course, Islam were to take different paths.

And it was a disaster of even greater magnitude than that of September 11, the sack of Rome by the Goths in 410, that led Augustine to reconsider the relationship between politics and religion. In the 390s, in the wake of the Theodosian adoption of Christianity as the official religion of the Empire, Augustine had been seduced by a form of Christian triumphalism that bound together state and church in the realisation of God's will. In the wake, how-

ever, of the great disaster that was to change his world forever, Augustine was forced to look again at the relationship
between the political world and the religious world. His
answer was the assertion that there were two cities, that of
man and that of God, and that earthly empires come and
go, unlike the eternal kingdom. At the same time this
involved the rejection of human perfectionism and the
recognition that human beings had to face the task of
living in this world and creating both order and a measure
of justice in the face of sin and their failings.

The heritage of Augustine is that there is both hope
and sin, but the hope will not be realised through human
contrivance by creating some sort of ideal Christian state.
Human beings must live in the world and seek justice, but
they are not in essence political beings, as Plato and Aris-
totle had believed. Politics is a human activity but it is
grounded in human imperfection; it has no special divine
sanction and it is an essentially secular activity.

Ancient cities, including Athens and Rome, had
brought together politics and religion. For the citizens of
these cities they were simultaneously the seat of politics
and sacred spaces. The city brought together the above and
the below. Augustine consummated a tendency within
Christianity to separate out the two. Christians were spread
across many cities; their sacred space was the Body of
Christ, the Christian community itself. Marcel Gauchet
argues that such a separation had been happening ever
since the creation of the earliest states, but it has only been
in the West that it has come to fruition with the creation
of a fully secular realm of politics.

Only in the West did politics become a fully

autonomous activity. Unlike any other civilisation the West is a political civilisation. But from Augustine onwards it has also had to face the essentially paradoxical nature of secular politics as an activity carried out by imperfect beings and limited in what it can achieve. In a fallen world political action seeks justice while yet knowing that true justice is not of this world. Political action in search of the good may require that the participant in such action acquire dirty hands. Even with the best of intentions the evil that lies within humanity's fallen nature cannot be avoided.

Such problems have been faced by some of the major political theorists of the West as they have striven to understand the nature of secular politics. Machiavelli was the first of these as he struggled with the problem that there might be times when evil means have to be used to achieve good ends. Hobbes clearly saw that human beings left to themselves would eventually create a state of war. If we are to live lives of peace and security then there must be order. The excesses of human nature, including those of murdering other people in the name of religion, must be restrained by an essentially secular political order.

Secular politics is a necessary activity, we need it just as we need good drains. It can also be a sordid activity that should not be glorified or invested with dreams of divine sanction. Many of the traditions of liberalism have inherited this balanced picture of politics that derives ultimately from Augustine. In particular this is the case with the variety of liberalism that emerged out of the sceptical Enlightenment and is associated with Montesquieu, Hume and the American Federalists. It is a form of liberalism that insists on checks and balances, constitutions, and the separation of powers as means of making politics work in the face of human weakness, so that justice can be pursued without political action being accorded an over inflated importance.

Western civilisation in the modern age has also seen attempts to bring heaven and earth back together again based on a desire to return to a pre-Augustinian idea of politics. The post-Enlightenment secular world that no longer believes in Heaven has sought to make politics into a form of substitute religious activity through which heaven can be realised on earth. Many nineteenth and twentieth century radicals, including Marx, saw the answer as a return to the Greek *polis*. Greek political man became a utopian ideal to be realised in the future. These radicals have an idealised picture of human beings as creatures who realise their true nature through politics. The consequence has been an excessive faith in the power of politics to achieve human redemption combined with the loss of an appreciation of the morally ambiguous and paradoxical qualities of political activity. In its place a Manichean morality has emerged that divides the world up into two camps, progressives and reactionaries. This Manicheanism judges all human actions according to whether they aid or retard certain 'progressive' political goals.

This has led in turn to the increasing politicisation of large parts of our existence, as almost any human activity can be thought of, mistakenly, in political terms. Even worse, with the spread of Western civilisation this disease has been exported to many parts of the world. Too many people in too many parts of the world now believe that politics holds the key to human improvement. While it may be true that we cannot escape politics it is also true that we should not expect it to do too much for us. Instead we have in the modern world excessive expectations of politics, though, in a half forgotten memory of the Augustinian heritage, this is often balanced by disgust at the reality that it involves.

September 11 should be considered as a wake up call. Far too many of us have been caught basking in the reflected glory of the fall of communism and the apparent triumph of liberal and capitalist values. The Kingdom did truly seem to be at hand, the end of history would see a liberal and democratic paradise emerge. We were deluded into thinking that perhaps political action might offer up redemption. We are like Augustine. We thought the modern equivalent of the Christian Empire had been achieved, and we have had to be jolted back into reality by a harsh and cruel event.

So, like Augustine we need to think clearly about the nature of politics and their place in the world. My thoughts on this matter run as follows:

1. Liberalism is not a redemptive doctrine. Instead it is the most appropriate political approach in a world inhabited by imperfect humans. There is no doubt that politics is a necessary human activity. We should try to pursue justice, and I believe that liberalism is the doctrine most likely to achieve this aim because of its emphasis on restraining human excess through such means as checks and balances, and because it has as its central focus individual responsibility. Market forces may not be a recipe for

perfection, but if our goal is a peaceful and prosperous world they are far more likely to achieve it than a politics based on redemption and the pursuit of perfection. This is because the pursuit of perfection brings out the worst in human nature; men and women become ready to use uncivilised means when they believe themselves to be the vehicles of a necessary and absolute truth.

2. Politics involves both good and evil. There are no absolutes in the secular world of politics, only choices between relative goods and evils. Under such circumstances a Manichean morality is especially dangerous as it works to distort our picture of reality. There must be order in the world, and governments must take actions to ensure that order. Those of a Manichean disposition condemn America as an imperialist state, as something evil because it does not live up to their vision of perfection.

As America is the most powerful country in the world it is inevitable that she will play a role in many parts of the world, and that role may be described as imperial. Yet of all the imperial states of the last one hundred years America is far and away the most benign. Think of other imperial states such as Hitler's Germany, Stalin's Russia or Mao's China. And America has been benign because it is essentially a liberal state that was founded on principles that sought to restrict power. We should be thankful that it was America and not the Soviet Union that won the Cold War.

Yet America, like all political entities, makes mistakes, gets its hands dirty and sometimes does unpalatable things with which we may not agree. There is a need to recognise that this is the case because of the nature of power and human politics in an imperfect world. This does not mean that we should excuse such excesses of power, only that we should recognise that politics is a morally ambiguous activity and that we are foolish to invest too much hope in it.

3. We need a realist politics that acknowledges its limitations while also recognising, like Augustine, that we should do what we can to create a more just world. The road to such a world, however, is not through fanaticism, fundamentalism, or dreams of perfection. What we all want is a world in which peace is the general rule and violence and war are kept to a minimum. This means, I believe, a world that recognises liberal principles that encourage individualism while restricting excesses of power. It is a secular world but one in which individuals are free to practise their religion but not to impose their religious beliefs on others. Good government based on liberal principles and commerce remains the most likely way of achieving a reasonably peaceful world.

When Augustine proclaimed his doctrine of the two cities he was seeking to disentangle the Church from the contingency of political institutions. In so doing he helped to bring into being a secular understanding of politics that has been central to Western civilisation. Politics is necessary but limited in what it can achieve. In the wake of September 11 we need once again to recognise the centrality of these insights if we are to continue to lead civilised lifestyles. When politics is appropriated by religious fanaticism and the desire to achieve redemption or perfection it becomes a tool of destruction that annihilates both order and justice.

Enemies in the Household

Sean Regan

> Do not suppose I have come to bring peace to the earth.
> It is not peace I have come to bring but a sword.
> And I have come to set a man against his father, a
> daughter against her mother, a daughter-in-law against
> her mother-in-law. A man's enemies will be those
> of his own household.
>
> *Matthew 10: 34-36*

> When two intelligences meet, the
> lower always pulls the higher down.
>
> *Emile Zola*

While events surrounding the death of Princess Diana and the terror of September 11 might appear to have nothing in common — other than providing an extended photo opportunity for Mr Tony Blair — measured reflection suggests they are equal if different manifestations of a

---

Sean Regan *trained in philosophy, politics and economics. He has worked as an academic, policy adviser, editor and journalist in Australia and overseas. Both his publications and professional contracts have covered a wide range of political persuasions. Currently he is a Canberra-based analyst and writer for a peak non-government organisation.*

new socio-political phenomenon to which those of us still reluctant to climb the moral high ground should pay the closest attention.

It is best explained with reference to the earlier episode. The outpouring of public grief that followed the fatal tunnel crash was, by all accounts, unprecedented. Even the notoriously buttoned-up English for once allowed their emotions full rein, weeping openly in the streets, hugging total strangers as the hearse passed by and abjuring centuries of deference to force the Windsors to honour the people's princess in the people's way. No other state funeral had aroused anything like the passionate intensity of this: neither for other members of royalty, national heroes like Winston Churchill nor even characters on *Coronation Street*. To an outsider, the spectacle was disconcerting, intriguing and strangely poignant.

The other side of the coin was less attractive. What the *Spectator*'s editor, Boris Johnson, has called the 'militant mourning' of the period dictated viciousness as much as unity. Those who, for whatever reason, failed to appreciate the full metaphysical significance of Diana's death were well advised to keep very quiet indeed. There were reports of individuals being reviled, spat on and beaten if they dared say a word out of place. In one instance, a carriage-load of patriots turned on a hapless rail commuter for making a weak joke about the crash – of the sort England's yeomen make every day about Afghanis or AIDS sufferers in workplace, pub and home. Monolithic sorrow overrode all, precluding not only bad taste, disaffection and criticism but also indifference.

Though the cause and circumstances were dramatically

different, there has been a comparable reaction throughout the West, but primarily in the United States, since September 11. This is not, obviously, to draw a direct analogy between the accidental death of a royal idol and the premeditated slaughter of thousands of innocent people. What nevertheless holds true of both cases is that the boundaries of acceptable public opinion, temper and behaviour were altered, such that a good deal of what was previously tolerated, if not lauded, is now forbidden, and vice versa. From the shelving of Hollywood disaster and splatter films to an almost total ban on humour and the final triumph of the civil rights movement in the fusion of black and white loathing of the towelheads, American life has changed, if not forever, then certainly the foreseeable future. Far more than in the case of the English, indeed explicitly so, national sentiment and policy are grounded in two mutually reinforcing claims: We are in the right. And those not with us are against us.

Towards a new paradigm

From the disinterested perspective of statistical metaphor, what both sets of events display is a disturbance in the normal distribution or Bell Curve of public opinion to resemble something closer to a graph of fee-paying students' course results. The bulk of respondents are no longer to be found in the middle range but are bunched towards the right, with the median displaced from its usual centre. Thus while before September 11, some 60–75 percent of Americans might have been in favour of the death penalty, now the figure is more like 85–90 percent. The average person has reassessed her values, the silent majority converted – and the logic is entirely visceral. As with those who failed to share in Britain's mass lamentation, anyone reckless enough to voice misgivings about the new way of doing things is ipso facto bordering on treason. In tandem with that (the causal relationship is complex) the government is free to introduce a raft of emergency measures and legislation it could never get away with in normal times, such as the introduction of closed military commissions to try suspected terrorists with no right of legal representation or appeal.

The excuse, of course, is that these are not normal times. America, Britain, Australia and all other countries who are with us are at war with those who are not, even if only a few to date, including the Japanese, have actually taken up arms. The corollary is that the new values and measures will only be temporary, since by definition they are not normal. The mourning over Diana could not last and the unthinkability of 'closure' on the popular taste for character assassination meant she would shortly be replaced by other, albeit more transient, figures from the peculiar world of celebrity. And as her face was gradually displaced from the covers of women's magazines, so the British people returned to their usual condition of lethargic resentment. Similarly, in liberal democracies, with war. Internment, for example, has only ever been justified as a matter of exigency, whether in international or civil combat. Locking people up because of their ethnicity, religion, citizenship or political views is, in peacetime, simply not done. The Bell Curve of ordinary Western public culture permits security, the genetic lottery and freedom of expression to coexist. Were this not so, many more people would be objecting to the pre-emptive restrictions on liberty which governments and super-governments – notably the European Union – always have ready and waiting to decree at the first available opportunity.

But what if war or a state of siege were to become, or seem to become, permanent? What if, one way or another, the abnormal conditions became, or could be made to appear, normal? Again, this would be tolerated, though with increasing resistance, so long as the evidence could be made to support it. The Bush administration has candidly declared that its war on terrorism is not an ordinary sort of war and may take years or even decades to reach an acceptable conclusion. Granted the hyperbole – like poverty, drugs or disease, terrorism is not something you can wage a successful war against – this is a reasonably honest statement about the intended duration of the emergency measures, which can be tested against forthcoming experience and subjected to the usual, flawed safeguards of democratic process. Should that experience be such that a majority of people come to accept the now abnormal conditions as normal, then the Bell Curve will be re-established, but with a different set of defining values. (To continue with the academic analogy: when all students are fee-paying the majority will again range from C- to B+.) The best known example of such readjustment is the painless manner in which the bureaucratic controls imposed in Britain during World War II, condemned at the time by Evelyn Waugh and other arch Tories as near-totalitarian, formed the basis of the postwar welfare state. With the more draconian regulations removed or eased, most Britons until the eighties were more than happy to live in what was to a considerable extent a command economy and paternalist society, as are most Scandinavians today. It was a choice more or less freely made on the basis of more or less forthright argument and evidence.

There is, however, another, less direct way to re-engineer normality, of its nature less honest (though making much of the word 'transparent') and more than arguably pernicious. This involves not a return to a Bell distribution on the basis of new or modified values, but a continual adjustment of the abnormal peak, depending on the topic and hysteria to hand. Thus on one day on one particular issue the peak could be way to the right of the graph; on another, way to the left. It might now and again be seduced by negative attractors; and on rare occasions even resemble the Bell Curve itself. It is a distribution pattern for the era of chaos theory. Embodying all the shades of irrationalism against which argument and evidence are futile, it has a far greater potential than warspeak to engage in permanent dislocation. As yet the template does not have a name. But in view of the bathos, special pleading and shiftiness on which it so heavily depends, as well as the man's central self-casting in both defining moments of our recent past, we might venture to call it the Blair Curve.

There are, obviously, other ways of depicting this instance of the fashionable art of 'sampling'. Psephologists have for some time been pointing out the obsolescence of traditional political affiliations and their replacement by fluid coalitions of otherwise disparate interests. Sociologists have drawn our attention to the disruptive influence of identity politics and the 'new social movements'. And in the *Australian*, Paul Kelly is in the throes of anatomising the

early-twenty-first century paradigm of parliamentary gov-
ernance. Though all are agreed that the centre cannot
hold, and that this will have a profound effect on the
coherence of democratic politics, they fail to capture the
heart of the show: which is, appropriately enough, the
heart – along with anything else that can be press-ganged
to still the warnings of the head. It is the sheerest emotionalism.

Two caveats must be made here, with important ram-
ifications in themselves. First, the underlying syndrome has
been maturing for some time; the death of Dodi Fayed's
girlfriend and the attacks in New York and Washington
were merely the catalyst for its fully fledged emergence
and consolidation. And secondly, movements in the Blair
Curve, though usually linked with opportunism, are fundamentally fired by a sincere conviction about whatever is
being advocated at the time. We are not talking about
hypocrisy or lies but a pathological form of speaking to
truth. Someone atop the Blair Curve not only cannot tell
a lie but has to chop down a few trees first in order not to
tell it.

The power of love

The first caveat has to do with what our more excitable
commentators bemoan as the legacy of the sixties. To an
extent they are right, but not in the way they believe or for
the reasons they adduce. The soft thinking that charac-
terises, say, most educational theory and practice was well
entrenched before the first hippy took his second step
towards corporate affluence. The fuzzy relativism now
underpinning mainstream social science and the 'critical'

humanities can be traced back to the grand anthropological tradition, if not the pre-Socratics. Political correctness itself was foreshadowed in the late Middle Ages in debates over the defining, and defining away, of sin. (And let us not forget the many cheesecloth enthusiasms nearly all of us now take for granted.)

What is consequential about the sixties – even if it does not make the period unique – is the manner in which an almost purely emotional take on life seeped first into the cultural and then the institutional liberal democratic mainstream. Love and peace were merely convenient labels for those who wanted easier sex and to avoid conscription. The critical development was intellectual, or rather anti-intellectual; and affected all segments of public life, no matter what the traditional or superficial differences. Argument yielded to opinion which in turn made way for feeling. The Cartesian *cogito* was transformed into a three chord blather. Self-expression took centre stage, but only if it was sufficiently infantile. Forget the difficult, oppressive business of reasoning. Just submit to the rhythm of your breathing, focus on the muscles in your left thumb and emote.

One of the most chilling images of recent years was that of the Blairs and Clintons cross-holding hands and leading an international conference singalong of the Beatles' 'All You Need Is Love'. One does not have to be enamoured of 'The Red Flag' or 'God Bless America' to sense that there was something seriously awry with these Baby Boomers' perspective on world affairs. Even the crowds in Islamabad or Riyadh burning effigies and railing against the Great Satan seemed to have a firmer grip on reality. Because, to state what should be the bleeding obvious but seems not to be, the very last thing you need in politics is love. Not because it is mushy or ephemeral or ridiculous, but because it substitutes magical for rational thinking. On its own terms, love is unconditional and irrational (as it remains when, inevitably, things turn sour). The very name of the loved one – worse, the loved ones, plural – suffices to shut out calm judgement and the possibility of doubt. The lover, relative, tribe, country or religion can do no wrong. Everyone else is, finally, dispensable. As emphasised in all the best love songs, it's you and me against the world, babe. And those not with us ...

What these people fail or refuse to realise is that the pluralist civil society that permits a Blair or Clinton to become its elected leader is the most unnatural system of order ever devised, its liberal democratic rule the most unnatural form of government. When it works (which is always imperfectly) it forces us to be honest with strangers, to trust banks with our money, to rely on testimony, to submit ourselves to a rule of law under which we must, in principle, be prepared to do to others only what we'd let them do to us. Put another way, liberal, civil society is the institutionalisation of anti-love. It requires people to confine their passions to the bedroom, church, synagogue, mosque and divorce court; or else to indulge them vicariously in mass entertainment and the licensed brutality of sport. Patriotism is encouraged, but not excessively so, lest it turn into xenophobia. Public and, to a great extent, private life is a constant battle against our hunter–gatherer selves, a series of generally unequal contracts and deals from which we may hope to gain a little comfort and dignity, and if we're lucky a year or two of contentment. It has nothing to do with idealism. Hobbes, not Jesus or Mohammed, Marx or Mill, is the one who underwrites whatever tranquillity we enjoy.

Within such an order there are obvious tensions, some the result of lingering pre-modern instinct, others an offshoot of the very Enlightenment traditions that made civil society possible in the first place. Mythical belief, for instance, is fully eliminated only in a handful of cases. Religion reappears as ideology, in profane notions of the chosen, the damned, the End of Days and, ultimately, some kind of earthly paradise. Above all, history and life have a purpose. And when one secular eschatology is discredited, another immediately takes its place. Hence in our day the common trek from Marxism to unbounded belief in the redemptive powers of the global market. True believers rarely have a sense of irony. Or as Orwell remarked, there is little point teaching a parrot new words.

Reason too can easily go off the rails. The hubris of natural scientists and the more ambitious technicians is rarely constrained by any reading of philosophy, literature or the other humane disciplines. When, like Professors Edward O. Wilson or Paul Davies, they stray into amateur epistemology or ontology, they simply make fools of themselves. But when their speculations underwrite actual practice and policy – in artificial intelligence, genetic engineering or missile defence systems, to take a few random examples – they become a poor man's Dr Frankenstein. The same applies *a fortiori* to social 'scientists' who, if not bound to some temporal religion, tend to put their penchant for ersatz mathematics into various forms of planning and proxy attempts at control. Given their head, economists, demographers and sociologists (not to mention their counterparts in architecture) can produce a Wonderland of rational delusions and bedlam, with results we might say were all too predictable had their creators ever bothered to learn from them.

Like our passions, these tensions have to be contained, since as long as we have a brain that is part-reptile and almost wholly ape they will not go away. The modest accomplishment of liberal, civil society – modern Western civilisation – is to have achieved that containment, tolerably well for most of the people most of the time. Which is also to say that the threads of civil order can very easily be broken, by war, resurgent communalism, zealotry or any other manifestation of primitive self-regard. From the sixties, civil order has been under constant threat from the purveyors of emotionalism, those who denigrate reason itself in the name of some higher good, particularly in the education system (at all levels), the communicative arts and government. Between the post-poststructuralist scholar introducing her charges to the joys of solipsism and the machine politician proactively repeating his focus group script in the guise of 'listening', there is a common interest in the erosion of rational debate. (One of the reasons we have never had to worry much about the *force de frappe* is that while the French may be cowardly, truculent and born collaborators, they still have a reasonable education system, at any rate for the governing orders.)

Though undoubtedly irritating, this development could until recently be ignored. When Tony and Bill were merely spouting their Lennonist rubbish at conferences or to impressionable academic groupies they were comparatively harmless (and at least they didn't choose 'Yellow Submarine' as their anthem). Once, however, their adolescent outlook actually began to influence policy they became dangerous. Guided by sentiment rather than sober or cynical calculation, they plunged into foreign adventures like the Bosnian conflict or the continuing bombardment of Iraq with all the foresight of a dog scenting a bone. It helped, of course, that they were also committed Christians, of the more robust variety. Apart from regarding those not with us as axiomatically against us, they took to heart Jesus' admonitions that brother will betray brother, the father his child, not to mention the tantalising promise, 'You will be hated by all men on account of my name'.

Of the two it is Blair who has proved the more belligerent. Having had personal experience of the draft, Clinton resisted committing ground troops to the Bosnian campaign. By contrast, Blair, from a generation most of whom had not even heard of National Service, was itching for a proper fight. In the event, the bigger escapist won, but only after fending off a snappy campaign of bleating from his younger political brother. With the advent of George W. Bush – a country rather than soft rock kind of Baby Boomer – and then September 11, the Prime Minister was able to indulge his Churchillian fantasies to the full, without the battle scars, political humiliations or whiskey. The Blair Curve had found its historic moment.

Opportunism transcended

The second caveat has to do with sincerity and opportunism. There can be no doubt that many individuals and institutions took advantage of September 11 to further interests or causes they would otherwise have found it very difficult if not impossible to pursue. The most obvious instance is the airline company boards who used the bombings to make massive cuts in their labour force and explain away the dramatic loss in profitability which had been evident for some time and caused solely by managerial exorbitance. On a broader level, the terror attack provided a rationale for the global recession we were going to have anyway as a result of the e-commerce tulip mania of the mid to late nineties: a textbook case of magical thinking to begin with.

More important, however, for the general health of civil society is the opportunity September 11 gave the little Robespierres in our midst to impose the kind of curtailments on individual liberty they have always wanted to impose but since 1945 and, even more so, the collapse of European communism, had found it politically untenable to justify. The American response we have already mentioned. In Britain, the Government introduced a completely unnecessary Anti-Terrorism, Crime and Security Bill, which was only defeated in the House of Lords because the peers of the realm didn't think it went far enough. Within the greater Union, Europol has been revamped to combine law enforcement and intelligence information, enjoying both unlimited coercive powers (to check, for example, all individual electronic communications) and immunity from investigation by any elected parliament. If the Australian Government has yet to emulate such thoroughness, it is not because of popular dissent, more a question of time management. (There is a pretty well defined bunch of outsiders to get rid of first.)

A comparable window of opportunity has been opened in cultural affairs. For a variety of reasons, some of them admirable, the prejudice and irrational fears of 'the other' that make us such devoted members of family and tribe are normally kept in check once we go outdoors. Civil society has to base the identity and responsibilities of citizenship on impersonal criteria. Whatever we personally think or feel about members of a given race, colour or religion, we can't normally say or do anything about it in public, without facing certain consequences, legal or otherwise. Even those brave or rash enough to articulate their position overtly have to rely on a final appeal to some basic value of civil society, such as integration or freedom of speech. Since the attack on the World Trade Centre nearly all such reticence has gone by the board. Not only can terrorist or criminal profiling now be explicitly targeted at named ethnic or religious groups; so can popular sentiment. The fact that this was precisely one of the major objectives of the attack (and others like it to come) is conveniently ignored. Whatever the *casus belli*, its effects are the same. Mobs in the West are no more able to differentiate Islam from Moslem terrorists than mobs in the Middle or Far East can distinguish Western civilisation from undeclared territorial incursions and indiscriminate slaughter. Organising Ramadan dinners at the White House or stressing that some of your best party paymasters are Arab only serves to deepen the malevolence.

Among the intellectuals

On the ideological front also, recent events have been an Allahsend to certain erstwhile members of the 'left' who had long waited for an opportunity to recant, but whose pride kept them mouthing the appropriate platitudes while growling in the wings. Most celebrated of the new converts is Christopher Hitchens, the English *flâneur* who for years has camouflaged his evident realisation that socialism is bankrupt with the veil of lively attacks on such hypocrites as Clinton, Kissinger and Mother Theresa in the pages of *Vanity Fair*, *Vogue* and other favoured publications of the ex-Trotskyist classes. September 11 gave him the chance not only to denounce his former comrades as the 'fascist left' – thereby indicating a surprising or wilful ignorance about the historical and philosophical origins of fascism – but more importantly to claim his spiritual Green Card. America, he can now publicly blair, is a bastion of freedom and tolerance. Send me your lean and hungry, your tired and emotional …

To be fair, an alternative explanation is that Hitchens is totally confused. Three decades of affluent radicalism can do that to a man. In which case, he will be more than happy to slide up and down the Blair Curve, especially at $2.50 a word. For, to generalise a little, it is members of the intelligentsia who have shown themselves most adept over the past forty or so years at substituting emotion for reason while using the tools of reason to cover their ideological tracks. Commitment to any cause is essentially emotional – and, like a petulant footballer, always transferable. Reason alone provides only grounds for scepticism, except in the case of the self-defining truths of logic, mathematics or tautology (and even these, one gathers, are increasingly open to question). While in itself no justification for remaining totally uncommitted, it does suggest we could do worse than reflect on the emotional base of our convictions. When Hume argued that reason should be the slave of the passions, he was not suggesting we should be in thrall to any old passion. We may all, finally, be tribal in our thinking, but some of us eat our enemies, while others try to live with them. It does make a difference, even to relativists.

Australia's intelligentsia is no more or less clannish than others in the West, and considerably less vindictive than its counterparts in Paris, Berlin or New York, but it does have a weakness for schoolyard name-calling and ganging up. An approved technique is delation by intellectual association. Thus anyone who opposed intervention in the Vietnam civil war was either a person of unyielding principle or a traitor – as distinct from someone who had independently weighed up the arguments and come to the conclusion that intervention wasn't morally or strategically worth the candle. So too in the current climate, any criticism of United States policy – let alone the merest suggestion that America had in many respect brought September 11 on herself – is taken as proof positive that you are one or the good guys or bad guys, depending on the interlocutor's intellectual poison.

It is possible to be neither. We who feel a mild distaste for that country's puritanical, geographically challenged exhibitionism are no more anti-American than a liking for prosciutto makes us anti-Semitic. And the observation that if you continue to bomb places at will and flaunt your technological superiority, you will provoke a pitiless low-tech response is no more than an observation – and a fairly obvious one at that. As is the observation that American espionage, again for all its technological sophistication – indeed, largely because of it – is appalling. Such observations most certainly do not commit one to the moral position that the terror attack was somehow deserved. Yet it is precisely the conflation of these quite distinct arguments that packs against the 'left' have sought to establish. There are, of course, people on the 'left' who do believe the attack was justified and who are ardently anti-American. But it is fallacious to contend that any criticism of US policy, or aversion to hamburgers, thereby commits one to that moral or parochial position – any more than the cause of sound economic management commits one to gutter populism. Yet among the intellectuals you have to be either for or against, of one affective disposition or the other, in this pack or that. And even if you find both sides repugnant, you will be assigned to one of them by the other. Life's messiness must not intrude on the proper Blairite demarcations – which move, like the global peacemaker himself, in ways that are not so much mysterious as occult.

Intellectuals and the
Agony of the Left

The Cuckoo in the Nest

Peter Saunders

Karl Marx famously wrote that capitalism was 'producing its own gravediggers'. He was referring to the proletariat – the vast army of industrial workers brought into being by the spread of the factory system, who would one day become sufficiently numerous, militant and organised to overthrow the capitalist order and replace it with socialism.

It never happened, of course. In the century and a half since Marx penned his call to arms, the working class in all advanced capitalist countries has become both smaller and more prosperous. It may have been true in Marx's day that most industrial workers had nothing to lose but their chains, but it is certainly not true today. With our owner-occupied homes, our superannuation funds, and our ever-rising standards of living, nearly all of us have a real material interest in the continued vitality of the

Peter Saunders is the Director of Social Policy Research Programmes at the Centre for Independent Studies, and a Visiting Fellow at Macquarie University. He was previously Research Manager at the Australian Institute of Family Studies, and before that he was Professor of Sociology at the University of Sussex. He has held visiting positions at universities in Australia, New Zealand, Germany and the US, and is the author of ten books.

capitalist growth machine, and we are not about to slaughter the goose which provides us with the golden eggs.

There is, however, one group in society, many of whose members still hanker after the destruction of capitalism. This is the (predominantly public sector) intelligentsia.

Given their hatred of capitalism, the intellectual class has long been hostile to all things American, for the United States is the homeland of contemporary global capitalism. And given this long-standing hostility towards the United States, it should have come as no surprise that prominent members of this intellectual class reacted as they did to the events of September 11.

The intellectuals and capitalism

Nearly a century after Marx made his ill-fated prophecy about the revolutionary role of the proletariat, Joseph Schumpeter returned to the idea that capitalism was creating a class which would eventually turn around and destroy it. Unlike Marx, however, Schumpeter believed that the challenge would come from the intellectuals rather than the workers. And (again unlike Marx) his prediction has proved uncannily prescient.

In *Capitalism, Socialism and Democracy*, Schumpeter identified two developments which he thought were threatening capitalism's long-term future.

One was the growth of absentee ownership. The emergence of huge corporations meant that businesses were no longer in the hands of individual owners. Schumpeter believed that the faceless professional managers who had taken them over would never show the same commitment to them as the old owners had done, nor could they inspire the same personal loyalty from their workforces. 'Eventually', he concluded, writing of the future of the capitalist system of private property, 'there will be nobody left who really cares to stand for it'.

The second development was the growth of a new, educated class that has no direct responsibility for practical affairs, that is detached from the messy business of making profit, and that is actively hostile to the capitalist system. This class was the intelligentsia.

Long before our current generation of politicians stumbled upon the idea that knowledge and education are increasingly vital in generating national prosperity, Schumpeter recognised that capitalism was creating a new 'knowledge society'. More and more people were being employed to administer, manage, innovate, create, research or teach, and ever fewer were being employed actually to produce the goods. Even at the time when he was writing, it was evident to Schumpeter that one of the great growth industries of the future would be education, and that the new, educated class that was emerging would play a crucial role in social and political affairs.

He believed that this class would ultimately destroy the capitalist system and the bourgeois social order. This is because it was reared in a spirit of critique without responsibility.

Shocking an unshockable world

The restless spirit of critical inquiry which the early capitalist period had unleashed with such devastating effect against the traditional institutions of medieval Europe was, in Schumpeter's view, now being turned against capitalism itself. In the vanguard of this onslaught was the newly emerging, and increasingly large, intellectual class.

Intellectuals find their rationale in criticising received wisdoms and challenging existing systems of power. As Karl Popper understood, there is little point in research which merely confirms existing knowledge; the point is to criticise received wisdoms and to falsify propositions which have hitherto been taken as true.

Each generation of intellectuals therefore seeks to make its name and secure its living by knocking down orthodoxies handed down from the generations before it. This, of course, is healthy – up to a point. As John Stuart Mill argued in his essay 'On Liberty', the tendency for human beings intellectually to conform with those around them can result in a stagnant society in which nothing progresses, and we should therefore applaud the rugged free-thinker who is willing to 'step outside the envelope'.

The problem arises, however, when a whole class of people makes its living from being critical, for this creates perpetual critique of all the institutions on which the society depends. In his book *The Consequences of Modernity*, the British sociologist Anthony Giddens coined a new phrase to describe this process of perpetual critique. He called it 'reflexive modernisation', and he noted how deeply unsettling it is at an individual and a societal level, for it constantly upsets people's sense of 'ontological security'.

Today's intellectual class monitors, comments upon and casts critical judgement over every aspect of our society. Nothing is sacrosanct – not religion or the systems of ethics traditionally associated with it, nor the sexual morality of the bourgeois family, nor the capitalist market system with its emphasis on private accumulation of wealth and individual acquisitiveness. All the core values, beliefs and behavioural rules on which modern societies are founded get subjected to constant and unrelenting critique and scrutiny – not by a small group of free-thinkers on the margins of the society, but by a huge stratum of opinionated 'experts' who have taken up positions (in the media, in the schools and universities, in the professions) at its very centre, and whose influence on public life and public opinion is pivotal.

Just about the only core value which all members of this new intellectual class willingly endorse and defend is what Kenan Malik recently referred to in a *New Statesman* article as the 'freedom to shock'. Citing Edmund Burke's complaint that Tom Paine had sought to destroy in six or seven days what it had taken six or seven centuries to create, Malik ends his article: 'Paine had no time for custom, no reverence for the past, no notion of deference to authority. Would that we had a few more Tom Paines and fewer Edmund Burkes today'.

What Malik overlooks, however, is that Western universities are today crammed full with aspiring Tom Paines (albeit of a somewhat lesser intellect). Today's intelligentsia sees it as its duty to express 'critical' opinions. Impatient with the legacy of the past, and uncomprehending of the importance of stability and continuity in human affairs, they show disdain for the conventions and values of earlier generations, and they embrace a romantic identity as 'outsiders', 'rebels' and 'critics' of the existing social order. Like Malik, these intellectual 'free spirits' believe that their vocation is to shock – to challenge orthodoxies, under-mine traditions, open up conventions to critical scrutiny.

The tragedy of the Western intelligentsia at the start of the twenty-first century, however, is that all the ortho-doxies have already been challenged. Tradition today carries no sanctity. There is nobody left to shock. Indeed, the intellectual class has itself become a new, orthodox establishment, and the left has for some years now been much more conservative than the so-called 'new right'.

In an earlier period, intellectuals pitted their spirit of critical rationality against the myths and dogmas of the Church, but in a godless world, where priests are exposed as child molesters, vicars preach politics from their pulpits, and a leading Church of England Bishop has described the resurrection as 'a conjuring trick with bones', attacks on the Christian religion have ceased to offer intellectuals any opportunity for notoriety (and attacks on other faiths are ruled out by the intellectuals' self-imposed commitment to 'multiculturalism'). Satire has lost its *frisson* – we have heard it all before, and our senses have been dulled by the esca-lation in self-consciously scurrilous attacks on orthodox beliefs and behaviours. Art galleries now compete with each other to display sliced-up sheep in formaldehyde, crucifixes in jugs of urine, unmade beds scattered with used condoms, and stylised mosaic portraits of child mur-derers. In such a world, today's lumpen-intellectuals cast around in ever increasing desperation to find *something* that can still make us sit up and take notice.

Their chance came on September 11. When those two aircraft smashed into the twin towers of the World Trade Centre (horrible, fascinating, spellbinding images played over and over on our television screens), people throughout the western world reacted with revulsion and disbelief to what they saw. Fleetingly, an old-fashioned moral consensus was resurrected that day, a conservative gut reaction against the atrocity in Manhattan that reaffirmed our collective dedication to the values of individual liberty and basic human decency that centrally define the bourgeois world.

For many members of the intellectual class, this was too good an opportunity to miss. Here at last was something they could be shocking about. Here at last was a chance to challenge mainstream sensibilities.

Expansion of the public sector

The new intellectual class occupies many different niches in modern society, but most of the positions that they occupy are created and funded by governments. This is not a class that starves in its garrets and suffers for its beliefs, nor is it one that sustains itself by participating in some 'alternative' economy. Today's critical intellectuals mainly exist by drawing public sector salaries, and they make their names and reputations by biting the hand that feeds them.

The rise of the intelligentsia after World War II went hand-in-hand with the expansion of the public sector. In Australia, public sector employment (in Commonwealth, State and local government jobs) rose from 662,000 in 1950 to a high of 1,791,000 in 1986 – an increase of 170 percent (the total has subsequently fallen back slightly to 1,427,000 as a result of privatisation – see the *Australia Year Book*). Many of these employees belong to the new intellectual class that Schumpeter identified.

It has taken political analysts quite a long time to cotton on to the importance of this development, but in the 1980s, the British political scientist (and Marxist) Patrick Dunleavy began to see what it meant. In two *Political Studies* articles, Dunleavy showed that, while social class was losing its significance as a predictor of British voters' political alignments, the sector in which they were employed was becoming increasingly pertinent. While public sector employees tended strongly to support left-wing parties, those in the private sector tended to support the right. The result was that class divisions were becoming blurred, particularly in the middle class where a sharp political division was opening up between those who worked for the government and were paid out of tax revenues, and those who worked for private companies and were paid out of profits.

This new political cleavage is not only expressed in the way people cast their ballot. Membership and support for the so-called 'new social movements', such as feminism and green politics, is, for example, strongly concentrated among middle class public sector employees. Similarly, some of the strongest and most militant trade unions in western capitalist countries today are found, not among private sector manual workers, but in the public sector professions (and within these professions, it is those involved in Schumpeter's knowledge industry, such as the teachers, that are among the most strident – consider the sheer bloody-mindedness exhibited by groups like the Australian Education Federation or the British National Union of Teachers).

Why are the public sector middle classes drawn to the left? Two equally plausible explanations suggest themselves.

The first is that these people know which side their bread is buttered on: left-wing parties tend to favour increased public spending (including increased public sector wages and salaries) so public sector employees see these parties as representing their economic interests.

The second explanation is that people who incline to the left will often tend to seek out public sector employment, for this offers the chance to 'provide a public service'. State sector professionals work with people rather than things, they 'care' and exercise 'compassion' for those less fortunate, and their jobs (funded out of taxation on profits) allow them to shelter from the profit-seeking grubbiness of the capitalist system.

Both explanations are probably valid and they are mutually reinforcing. Idealistic young people who leave university wanting to change the world often gravitate towards public sector jobs, and this in turn strengthens their affinity for left-wing political agendas. The public sector intelligentsia is, therefore, a class that is profoundly anti-capitalist, both as a result of its early socialisation, and as a consequence of its daily practice, which is totally divorced from the private enterprise system.

The moral indignation of the intellectuals

In *The Fatal Conceit*, Friedrich Hayek makes the point that capitalism rarely inspires people. It is a system that works (and works extraordinarily effectively in delivering more and more goods to more and more people), but it lacks 'the vision thing'. This is because the capitalist market system works with little or no conscious human intervention or direction. There is no blueprint or grand plan; there are no levers to pull; and we do not really understand even now how it delivers the goods.

The Western public sector intelligentsia finds it difficult to identify with a system like this, for two reasons.

First, it renders them marginal and allocates them a rather peripheral role in human affairs. The capitalist system does not need visionaries to make it work, nor planners to give it direction. There is no need for a capitalist Lenin to ride a sealed train, nor any opportunity for a bourgeois Mao to lead a long march. This is a system on auto-pilot, and it has no final goal. There is no teleology, no inevitable historical end-point, no deliverance or salvation as there is in socialism. There is therefore no need for an intellectual priesthood to lead the way.

In the modern, globalised capitalist system, there is nothing much for a critical intelligentsia to do. They do not produce the wealth, and they are not required to change history. The system does not have much need for their insights and intelligence to make it function. Increasingly, they are used as mass producers of 'knowledge' or 'education' marketed in the form of commodities: something they resent as demeaning and inappropriate. University academics, for example, are now employed mainly to shepherd millions of largely uninterested adolescents through a hugely expanded and devalued system of mass higher education. This has come as a huge blow to their pride and sense of self-importance, and it has resulted in an unseemly rush to buy themselves out of their mundane university duties by pursuing government consultancies and government-funded research grants.

The second reason why the intellectuals cannot connect with the modern capitalist system is that it has no obvious 'moral logic' underpinning it and driving it forward. The intellectual class has grown up to value systems that are ordered according to some system of ethics. The capitalist system, however, is amoral. It is not designed to minister to the weak or redistribute to the poor (although these groups benefit from the growth that it generates much more than they ever benefited from the various socialist revolutions carried out in their name during the twentieth century). It is not even designed to reward the deserving, for it is indifferent to meritocracy just as it is to egalitarianism.

Robert Nozick has suggested in one of his *Socratic Puzzles* that one reason why the intellectual class is so opposed to the capitalist market system is that capitalism does not reward intellect as merit-worthy in and of itself. Throughout their early development within formal systems of education, intellectuals grow accustomed to attracting praise and winning prizes on account of their cleverness, but outside of the cloisters and the examination room they find that cleverness is not always and necessarily rewarded, and that people who take risks or who charm others or who work with their hands or who just strike lucky often end up more highly rewarded (with prestige as well as cash) than they are. This hurts (and it helps explain why groups like university academics and school teachers complain so frequently and so bitterly about their salary levels, comparing them with those in 'less meritorious' private sector jobs).

In contrast to capitalism, which delivers but cannot inspire, socialism inspires but cannot deliver. Those who live by ideas have found it hard to accept this practical failure. How can an idea as noble as socialism be jettisoned, just because it has never worked? The socialist dream of designing and engineering a 'better', more 'humane' and more 'rational' society has a strong hold on the imagination of left-wing intellectuals in the West, and they have found it difficult to come to terms with the reality that it has failed. They know that socialism is a 'better', more 'rational', more 'humanitarian' system than capitalism. It should have won, but it didn't. As Leonard Cohen succinctly expressed it in one of his 1990s songs: 'The war is over; the good guys lost'.

Bad losers (1) We have lost, but so will you

There are two ways in which Western public affairs intellectuals have come to terms with the defeat of the socialist vision and the triumph of global capitalism. In different ways they both involve turning capitalism's success against itself.

One is to take comfort in the belief that, although socialism crashed, the world capitalist system is also headed for disaster at some point in the future. The other is to assert that, although capitalism has triumphed materially, it has failed spiritually. Both arguments converge on a blistering critique of the United States.

The first argument suggests that capitalism's magical ability to keep growing will ultimately prove its comeuppance. This line is, of course, strongly associated with the green movement in its various forms, and it has been embraced by many sections of the intellectual class since the fall of the Berlin Wall, for it effectively recasts the old socialist dialectic in a new guise.

One of the most influential works of social theory in the 1990s, for example, was Ulrich Beck's *The Risk Society* which argued that economic growth and technological development have brought us to a point where the chemical, nuclear, environmental and genetic risks entailed in new investments are literally incalculable and therefore uninsurable. Gradually, the world's population is coming to understand this, and to resist it. The longer the capitalist system is allowed to continue, the greater this awareness and resistance will become, and at some point the 'modernist' project itself will have to be abandoned.

This idea – that the apparent success of global capitalism is actually contributing to its eventual collapse – is popular among members of today's intellectual class, and it crops up in various different forms. In Australia, for example, Richard Eckersley suggested in a *Family Matters* article in 1998 that 'progress' has become self-defeating. The richer we become, the unhappier we feel, for we have reached the point of diminishing returns from economic growth. Citing statistics on youth unemployment, youth suicide, crime, drug abuse and divorce, as well as attitudinal data suggesting that most young people are disillusioned about the way their society is headed, Eckersley suggested that modern society is 'increasingly hostile to our well being' and that the economy needs to be 'driven by different values towards different ends'.

The first response of the intellectuals to the triumph

of capitalism has, therefore, been to dismiss it as a Pyrrhic victory. Capitalism is piling up huge dangers that it cannot control. Capitalism can deliver growth, but more growth is the last thing we need.

The country against which all these critiques are sooner or later directed is the United States. In the face of all this intellectual angst about environmental collapse and individual malaise, America remains proudly wedded to consumerism. Throughout the 1990s the American economy grew at a record rate, delivering full employment, low inflation and rising standards of living. This was like a slap in the face to the Western intelligentsia, for not only had the US successfully seen off socialism, but now it was proving resolutely indifferent to the new environmentalist creed that had replaced it. The refusal to sign up to the Kyoto protocol on climate change generated enormous anger and hostility among Western intellectuals who were convinced that we are headed straight for oblivion unless we (led, of course, by them) do something dramatic and do it fast. In their eyes, the US was being typically arrogant, selfish, stupid and short-sighted – but without America, it was obvious that nothing effective could be done.

Bad losers (2) We have lost, but we are still superior to you

The second response to the triumph of global capitalism from the intellectual class has been to focus on 'higher things'. According to this line of thinking, capitalism might be good at putting clothes on our backs and food in our bellies, but it does nothing to sustain the soul.

This line of thinking does not, let us hasten to add,

represent a return to religious faith, for the intelligentsia still wants nothing to do with gods and demons, and its commitment to ethical relativism makes it unwilling to tolerate any source of moral authority other than its own. The appeal to higher virtues involves an assertion of 'humanistic' values, not religious ones, and it is grounded in a deep-seated sense of cultural superiority.

Nowhere does this sense of cultural superiority come out more clearly than in the intellectuals' responses to Hollywood and American popular culture. Notwithstanding all the recent discussion of post-modernism and 'post-Fordism' in Western intellectual circles, capitalism is still fundamentally a mass system. It creates mass products for a mass market, and its cultural products are in this respect no different from any other. The epitome of this culture industry is Hollywood.

Hollywood throws millions of dollars into movies intended to do little more than entertain people. At its annual Oscars ceremony, Hollywood refers to what it does as 'motion picture art', and its highly-paid stars refer to themselves as artists, but it measures its success by box office receipts. Hollywood output is generally lightweight and 'superficial' – you consume a Hollywood film along with a bucket of popcorn, and within hours you have forgotten what you saw. Not for Hollywood the raw exposés of working class life so favoured by British film-makers, nor the deeply cerebral examinations of love and death indulged in by the French. Hollywood is not really interested in telling us about the meaning of life or putting us in touch with our soul. It just hopes to fill a couple of hours pleasurably. And it turns out that is just what most of us want at the end of a long day.

The intellectual class *hates* Hollywood (even though some Hollywood 'artists' like to think of themselves as part of the intelligentsia). It prefers inaccessible 'art-house' cinema, created by fringe directors, filmed with hand-held cameras in black-and-white, usually involving sub-titles, the more impenetrable the better. The reason for this has to do with the distinction between 'high' and 'low' culture.

In his book *Culture and Anarchy*, the mid-nineteenth century poet and educationalist, Matthew Arnold, defined high culture as beauty and intelligence – 'sweetness and light'. High culture consists of 'the best that has been thought and said in the world' – things like Shakespeare's plays, Mozart's music, or Rembrandt's paintings. These works come close to perfection, and according to Arnold, they are unquestionably among the highest cultural achievements of humankind. He had no hesitation in claiming that this judgement holds across all times and all places, for Arnold was no relativist.

Today's intellectual class feels extremely uncomfortable with claims like this, for not only do they contradict its insistence on relativism (the belief that no set of ideas or beliefs can be said to be better than any other), but they also fly in the face of its commitment to multiculturalism (the myth that all cultural practices are of equal worth and that they cannot be judged against any external, objective standards of worth). For some members of today's intelligentsia, Shakespeare, Mozart and Rembrandt (among other notable 'dead white males') should command no more respect or reverence within the school and university syllabus than, say, the contemporary outpourings of black 'ghetto culture', 'women's culture', or whatever. For them, the distinction between 'high' and 'low' culture is just one more way in which an elite has tried to impose and maintain its power and domination.

The intelligentsia therefore indignantly denies the possibility of distinguishing a 'high' culture from a 'low' one – but with one notable exception. When it comes to American culture in general, and to Hollywood in particular, the intelligentsia is prepared to make a judgement. American culture is unambiguously *inferior* and Hollywood is its dominant medium. American television and film output is *low-brow* and in this it merely reflects the naïve, superficial, unchallenging, predictable, banal and commercially contaminated culture which spawns it.

The intellectuals despise almost everything about American popular culture. They are scornful of American politics, dismissing hugely popular Presidents such as Reagan and George 'Dubya' Bush as dullards. They wince at America's continuing devotion to religion and cannot begin to understand how so many people can take all these tub-thumping television revivalist preachers and happy-clappy holy rollers so seriously. They are appalled at American educational standards and at the shameless ignorance and indifference displayed by so many Americans towards the world beyond their shores. They are indignant that most American states have the nerve to continue to gas and electrocute and administer lethal injections to their convicted murderers when other Western countries abandoned such 'barbaric' practices years ago. They are furious on behalf of America's poor and its racial and ethnic minorities that the welfare system now requires that poor people get jobs while the legal system insists on locking up those who break the law. They are convinced that most Americans (Ivy League professors apart) are just cowboys at heart, and they mock their cherished 'right to bear arms' for having created a society with the highest homicide rate in the Western world. And (*Seinfeld* and *Frasier* apart) they shudder at American television.

How (the left intelligentsia repeatedly asks itself) can a country like this be so successful? How can a country that is so obviously *anti-intellectual* and *uncultured* and *unplanned* and *uncivilised* and downright *dumb* dominate the world so easily, not only economically, but politically, militarily and culturally? How can a country that ignores so much of what left intellectual opinion takes as self-evidently the right way to organise public affairs still come out on top every time? Every day that America survives and thrives, its very existence mocks almost everything that the public sector intellectual class cherishes and passionately believes to be true.

The Cassandra tragedy

There can be few things so frustrating as to be convinced that one is right, yet to find no-one else interested in listening to you. Like Cassandra, who was doomed to tell the truth but find nobody prepared to believe her, the intellectual class today genuinely and sincerely believes that it is right, yet it finds that its warnings and its criticisms go constantly unheeded.

This kind of frustration breeds hatred. America is hated because it so successfully treads the 'wrong' path and keeps taking the rest of the world along with it.

The explanation that the intellectuals themselves offer for why America remains so popular and attractive to almost everybody apart from themselves is that we have all been seduced by its 'glitz and glamour'. We have all been fooled by appearances.

In his comparison of American and 'Rhine-model' capitalism, for example, Michel Albert (*Capitalism Against Capitalism*) leaves us in no doubt about which is the self-evidently better system. The European Union has a better welfare system than the US, it has lower levels of personal debt, it has a more consensual system of running industry, it cares more for the environment – yet Albert recognises that the American system will almost certainly triumph over the European model. Why? Because America markets its image so successfully through rock music and sport and (most of all) Hollywood.

We have encountered this sort of argument before. Drawing on a mish-mash of Marx and Freud, Herbert Marcuse argued in *One-Dimensional Man* that capitalism does not and cannot meet genuine and deep human needs for self-fulfilment and self-realization. It nevertheless gains the support of the 'masses' by literally selling itself. It cannot provide people with true happiness (their 'real needs'), but it can provide cars, refrigerators and holidays on sunny beaches ('false needs'). It therefore indoctrinates people (through advertising and other means) to want the commodities that it is capable of supplying, and it diverts their attention from the deeper things that they need but that it can never supply.

Whether or not they agree with Marcuse in the detail, left intellectuals today tend to argue along precisely these lines about America. America survives, they believe, through a sleight of hand, and they are desperate to expose the fraud (or as the gurus of the English literature, sociology and cultural and media studies departments in our universities would have it, to 'deconstruct' the dominant 'discourse').

The longer this goes on, the more angry and frustrated they become at their inability to strip away the glitz and reveal the true essence of American capitalism, militarism and exploitation that lies behind it. The hatred of America felt by the intellectual class of most Western countries is, in short, a hatred born of a righteous sense of defeat, and in this sense, it bears some comparison with the sources of the 'Muslim rage' against America famously analysed by Bernard Lewis. In both cases, the anger grows out of the assumed superiority of their beliefs combined with a recognition of their failure to prevail over an inferior adversary.

Of course, left intellectuals would never hijack an airliner and fly it into the World Trade Centre. They are too sensitive for that, and all the intellectuals I know were genuinely horrified by the events they saw relayed over their TV screens on September 11. Nor, despite their passionate concern for the interests of 'exploited' and 'oppressed' peoples in developing countries, could many members of the Western intellectual class bring themselves actually to support the likes of Osama bin Laden and his Taliban allies in their battle against America. The suppression of women's rights and the imposition of religious orthodoxy by the Taliban regime was too strong a medicine for most western intellectuals to swallow, although most of them did oppose the American war against Afhanistan that followed the September 11 attacks.

Despite these misgivings, many intellectuals still found it difficult to suppress an illicit and irrational feeling of *Schadenfreude* when they came to reflect on the events of September 11. Of course, they began to say among themselves, it was awful what happened to all those unfortunate people who were killed. But didn't America have it coming? What had happened in New York and Washington was really no worse than what America had dished out over the years in Iran or elsewhere in the Arab world. And wasn't there a sort of 'justice' in the fact that America was on the receiving end for once? Indeed, was there not a sense that America had brought this upon itself; that America was really to blame for its own suffering?

For an intellectual class whose members had seen their visions trampled by American triumphs, and who had tried for so long and with such conspicuous lack of success to expose what they saw as the 'fraudulent' appeal of America's global success, it did not seem unreasonable, just this once, to break the habit of a lifetime and agree to blame the victim.

September 11 and the End of Ideology

Keith Windschuttle

In the last week of September, the Italian Prime Minister, Silvio Berlusconi, made an extraordinary statement. He said:

> We must be aware of the superiority of our civilisa-
> tion, a system that has guaranteed well-being,
> respect for human rights and – in contrast with
> Islamic countries – respect for religious and political
> rights.

The minute he had uttered these words, a bevy of European politicians rushed to denounce him. The Belgian Prime Minister, Guy Verhofstadt, said: 'I can hardly believe that the Italian Prime Minister made such

---

Keith Windschuttle is an historian and publisher who is a frequent contributor to The New Criterion and Quadrant. He is author of The Killing of History: How Literary Critics and Social Theorists Are Murdering Our Past *(Encounter Books, 2000) and five other books. He is publisher of Macleay Press, Sydney, and is a former academic who taught history and social policy at the University of New South Wales and other Australian universities.*

statements'. Spokesman for the European Commission, Jean-Christophe Filori, added: 'We certainly don't share the views expressed by Mr Berlusconi'. Italy's centre-left opposition spokesman Giovanni Berlinguer called the words 'eccentric and dangerous'. Within days, Berlusconi was forced to withdraw.

It is true that the statement could have been more diplomatically timed, made as it was while American officials were trying to put together an anti-terrorist coalition of Islamic allies. But there is little doubt it would have generated just as many denials no matter when it was uttered. The statement was extraordinary because Western superiority, though patently obvious to everyone, has become a truth that must not be spoken.

The chief reason is the prevailing ideology of the Western intelligentsia. Today, the leading opinion makers in the media, the universities and the churches regard Western superiority as, at best, something to be ashamed of, and at worst, something to be opposed. Until thirty years ago, when Western intellectuals reflected on the long-term achievements of their culture, they explained it in terms of its own evolution: the inheritance of ancient Greece, Rome and Christianity, tempered by the Renaissance, the Reformation, the Enlightenment and the scientific and industrial revolutions. Today, however, such thinking is dismissed by the prevailing intelligentsia as triumphalist. Western political and economic dominance is more commonly explained in terms of its rivalry and aggression towards other cultures. Our success has purportedly been at their expense.

The intelligentsia widely regards Western success as

inherently sinful. Consequently, we are urged to redeem ourselves not only by changing our policies towards the non-West but also by acknowledging our sins and denying our superiority.

We are told to adopt the ethics of moral equivalence and cultural relativism. Under these rules, all cultures are equal though different. We are taught the postmodern rule that no culture can judge another because there are no universal standards. The most blatant recent example of this was expressed by the Reuter's News Agency. In response to September 11, it banned its reporters from using the term 'terrorists'. According to Reuters global head of news, Steven Jukes, 'one man's terrorist is another man's freedom fighter'.

According to this ideology, instead of attempting to globalise its values, the West should stay in its own cultural backyard. Values like universal human rights, individualism and liberalism are regarded merely as ethnocentric products of Western history. The scientific knowledge that the West has produced is simply one of many 'ways of knowing'. In place of Western universalism, we are told to accept the relativism of multiculturalism, a concept that regards the West not as superior but as simply one of many equally valid cultural systems.

Although presented with a gloss of tolerance and respect for other cultures, this position is inherently inconsistent. Its plea for acceptance and open-mindedness ceases when it comes to Western culture, whose history it regards as little more than a crime against the rest of humanity. We cannot judge other cultures but we must condemn our own.

This anti-Western, postmodern, multicultural, post-colonial intellectual edifice constitutes a true ideology: it is formidable in its comprehensiveness, in the number of intellectual fields it encompasses, and in the number of professional and public institutions it has successfully captured and whose agenda it now controls. With the demise of Marxism since the 1980s, it has emerged as its major ideological successor.

Although it is early days yet, one of the biggest losers from September 11 may well be this very intellectual mindset. It has become palpably clear to everyone *except* the current intelligentsia that you can no longer be a cultural relativist or a moral nihilist of the Susan Sontag variety.

Sontag wrote in the *New Yorker* on September 17:

> The voices licensed to follow the event [that is, press and TV news reporters] seem to have joined together in a campaign to infantilise the public. Where is the acknowledgement that this was not a 'cowardly' attack on 'civilization' or 'liberty' or 'humanity' or 'the free world' but an attack on the world's self-proclaimed super-power, undertaken as a consequence of specific American alliances and actions?

In other words, the ordinary public, the consumers of the media, are gullible children who, if they were better informed, would see their own country's responsibility for the terrorist attacks. This kind of comment drew the following sycophantic support from the Melbourne literary critic, Peter Craven, who wrote in the *Australian:* 'It's not hard to admire Sontag's stance ... It is so cool, so bracing, it stares so bravely over the heads of the mob'.

Of course, by 'the mob', Craven means those ordinary Australians who constitute the citizenry of this democratic nation. To him and to Sontag, such people are plainly objects of contempt.

However, since September 11, the most visible political development on the left has not been the series of half-hearted, poorly attended anti-war marches. The most obvious phenomenon has been the split between the liberal left and the radical left. The liberal left is pro-American; the radical left is still anti-American.

A number of celebrity leftists have very publicly jumped this fence. The best known is Christopher Hitchens, who called bin Laden 'fascism with an Islamic face' and has since been denouncing his former colleagues in similar terms. He has even announced he has given up socialism. Todd Gitlin, one of America's celebrity revolutionaries of the sixties, has begun flying an American flag from his balcony. Harvey Kaye, a Marxist American historian who writes for the *Times Higher Education Supplement*, also announced he had changed his ways and joined the liberal left. Even the Australian literary impostor, Helen Darville, said, when describing her response to September 11: 'I have watched, since that day, the cosy leftist pieties of my youth disintegrate'. For every public conversion of this kind there are bound to be many more private ones. While this development might be difficult to quantify just yet, it is very clearly detectable.

Some of this is, admittedly, sheer opportunism. For

instance, the first comments by the postcolonial literary critic, Edward Said, made no censure of the terrorists but said the Bush administration was engaged in 'inflamed patriotism and belligerent war-mongering'. But by the end of September, having seen which way the wind was blowing among his colleagues, he made some criticisms of the terrorists, calling their actions 'demonic' and 'bloody-minded', before going on to repeat the familiar radical left demands for Israel to retreat from Palestine and for the overthrow of the pro-American rulers of Arab states. Said added that people should 'discriminate' between Palestinian terrorism in Israel, which he found 'understandable', and the less acceptable Islamic terrorism against New York, where he lives.

Even Sontag, once she realised how widely detested her initial comments had made her, suddenly discovered patriotism. Abandoning her cool and deserting earlier devotees like Peter Craven, she told an interviewer in mid-October: 'I cry every morning real tears, I mean down the cheek tears, when I read those small obituaries that the *New York Times* publishes of the people who died in the World Trade Centre'. She added: 'And, no, I don't think we have brought this upon ourselves'.

However, not all of those who have changed their sentiments can have been opportunists of this kind. The terrorist attack forced every one with the capacity to think for themselves to do just that. In this situation, people really did have to ask where their loyalties lay, especially when so many of their compatriots died so horribly.

Terrorism does have an evil logic: it is a cathartic and a polarising phenomenon. It concentrates the mind and forces many people seriously to examine their allegiances. In the West from now on, this process will face the radical left, no matter how many academic and media outlets it still controls, with political and cultural isolation.

Most of the political activists, writers, artists and intellectuals on the left who repeated the chorus that America had only got what it deserved are plainly people who do *not* fit the category of those who could think for themselves about the matter. All of them could immediately slot September 11 into their own pre-existing matrix of morality, without its shaking any of the certainties on which their worldview was founded. This was because they remained creatures of the prevailing anti-Western ideology, which determined their responses.

In the wake of September 11, however, there is a real possibility that we may be seeing the last of this mode of thought. If the split between the radical left and the liberal left continues to widen, the radicals may indeed be among the major losers from these terrible events. And if this particular ideology does collapse completely, this may well be momentous. For once the postmodern, multicultural, postcolonial mode of thought has gone, there is no alternative anti-Western ideology waiting in the wings to replace it. If all this comes to pass, we may be witnessing the often predicted, but yet to be realised, 'end of ideology' in the West.

Nonetheless, intellectual edifices of this kind, no matter how disconnected they become from the mainstream of their society, never fall entirely of their own accord. They still need to be pushed. Those who are opposed to this particular ideology have still got a lot of pushing and shoving left to do.

In the Land of the Deaf

Tim Blair

Before September 11, the World Trade Centre was visible from most anywhere in Manhattan and Brooklyn. Two weeks later, the first warning that you are approaching the site where the Twin Towers once stood comes from sound rather than sight.

It's a crackle of grit under your shoes. You're walking *on* the World Trade Centre, tiny particles of which were spread over miles of Manhattan in huge, boiling clouds as the buildings collapsed.

There are, of course, visual clues as well. Parked cars covered in death dust, their owners never to return; handmade posters on every wall, window, and parking sign, pleading for information on vanished friends, parents, or children; smoke rising from the pyre at Ground Zero; and the faint tremor in Jason Wong's exhausted hands.

Wong runs a physical therapy and massage clinic a few blocks from the WTC. Usually he caters to uptight

Tim Blair *is a former writer for* Time *magazine and the* Daily Telegraph*, and is a regular contributor to the* Australian Financial Review*, the* Age*, the* Australian *and the* University of Southern California's *Online Journalism Review.* He reported from New York City in the weeks following September 11.

businessfolk with bad backs or ricked necks. Since September 12, he and his staff have been working for free to treat WTC rescuers, firemen, and volunteers. Wong hasn't slept for days. Asked what the workers are telling him, he struggles, awfully. 'I cannot … the words aren't …' he begins. Then he punches his chest, hard. 'It's here that they feel it. This is where they hurt.'

Around the same time that Jason Wong was finding it so difficult to articulate the feelings of New Yorkers, *Sydney Morning Herald* columnist Peter FitzSimons offered a response to September 11. His advice to Wong, the families of the dead, and the West in general: get down on your knees and beg forgiveness. 'I think I speak for many over here when I say, "Hello. We are sorry",' wrote FitzSimons. 'We accept that such hate as drove the planes into the World Trade Centre towers can only have come from incredible suffering, and we are desperately sorry for that suffering, even if we are yet to come to grips with its specific cause.'

Apart from the 'Hello', I'd like to think that FitzSimons doesn't speak for many people at all. Certainly not coherent, rational people, who generally seek apologies from attackers rather than the attacked. At least FitzSimons has helped us understand just what that doomed student was up to in 1989 when he blocked a line of tanks in Tianamen Square; he was trying to say sorry for the 'incredible suffering' that must have prompted the murder of all his friends.

Has the Australian left ever abandoned logic so completely? To most people, the images beamed out of New York on September 11 were unambiguous: two jets com-

mandeered by madmen crashed into two gigantic buildings, killing thousands of innocent people. As seen by the
left, however, those monstrous towers rose up and swatted
brave freedom fighters from the sky. According to magistrate Pat O'Shane there is no evidence that suggests WTC
suicide pilot Mohamed Atta 'is/was a terrorist'. Well, I
guess not, unless you consider all those people he
killed/murdered in an act of terrorism. Bob Ellis is another
Atta-boy, writing in the *Canberra Times* that the attackers
were 'very brave and they did not run away'. Which, as we
all know, is a simple matter when you're aboard a jet airliner.

Ellis's article also contained one of myriad examples
to emerge after September 11 of what we might call
'politically-correct projection', whereby wishful anti-
Westerners attached all manner of decent motives to the
attack. The attack wasn't an 'act of madness', Ellis wrote. 'It
achieved a sane end, a real truce in Israel, and it powerfully
publicised the daily suffering of the Third World under the
unfeeling market capitalism of the First World.'

Thank you, multi-millionaire Osama bin Laden, for
instructing us on the evils of capitalism! The oppressors
within the World Trade Centre have surely learned their
lesson.

(Proving that clothes truly do maketh the man,
American leftist Michael Moore was as off-beam as his
shambling Australian doppelganger Ellis, claiming on September 12 that 'if someone did this to get back at Bush,
then they did so by killing thousands of people who DID
NOT VOTE for him! Boston, New York, DC, and the
planes' destination of California – these were places that

voted AGAINST Bush!' Good call, chubs. The terrorists began planning months before Bush had even been nominated.)

Newspaper letters pages were loaded with PC projection. Paul Collins, intellectual, of Pennant Hills, wrote that we wouldn't understand the horrific events at the WTC until we realise 'that the rest of the world lives in poverty so that we can have nice running shoes'. The same kind you use when you flee a jet? Darrell Greer, muppet, of Newtown, wrote that 'no-one has proved [bin Laden] was responsible' and sneeringly wondered if corporate America would sponsor the coming war: 'Would you like fries with that?' Darrell must have learned that line at his day job. David Lyons, plonker, of Hallidays Point, cast bin Laden in the role of EcoWarrior: 'The horrific attack on America may have been brilliantly planned and executed, but the planners and perpetrators are fools if they think this event will deter the world's greediest nation from its course of consuming most of the world's resources and being the world's greatest polluter'.

Yes, they *would* be fools to think that, David, mainly because that was never their aim. Dave's rudimentary bin Laden research obviously hadn't turned up the fact that his wealth came about through such things as highway construction. Bin Laden may be the worst human on earth, but at least he isn't an environmentalist.

Jif Morrison, cleaning product, of Clovelly, took the FitzSimons angle: 'To claim the latest outrage is an "assault on democracy" is being simplistic and divisive. A more constructive approach might be to address the grievances and inequalities that provoke such drastic behaviour'. Yes, like the inequalities between $50-million-dollar-man Osama and the workaday people his henchmen slaughtered.

By the way, who were those people in the WTC towers? They were the products of a violent, racist culture, according to Phillip Adams, who assembled a damning list of American crimes for a column in the *Australian*: rioting whites killed blacks in 1943; 39 blacks were killed by white mobs in 1917; Los Angeles burned following the Rodney King verdict; two million blacks were imprisoned during the war on drugs; and so on. Adams is confusing New York 2001 with Alabama 1963. He should examine the names of the WTC victims, which reveal a multiculturalism so extensive and diverse it makes Australia look like an 18-million member Von Trapp family: Gopu, Abad, Cho, Ahladiotis, DeFazio, Goldberg, Bakalinskaya, Doi, Economos, Bijoux, Agarwala, Gscaar, Carranza, Gjonbalaj …

Still, inequality is the root of all evil, according to the left, so the US is in the wrong simply for having more stuff. This doesn't explain why other poor nations haven't so far launched their own suicide attacks. And it doesn't explain acts of evil committed within poor nations, like Afghanistan. It's quite possible that the Taliban's destruction of the centuries-old Bamian Buddhas wasn't provoked by a wealth gap between the First and Third Worlds. And when Taliban officers stormed through Kabul's National Museum last year, smashing any art work bearing an image of a living thing – nearly 3,000 ancient artefacts were ruined – dismayed museum staff didn't report any complaints from the Taliban about poverty. It would be interesting to read a leftist analysis of these events. So far, we've not seen a word.

This is a terrible thing to say, but at times it seems as though, for all their concern over global events, the caring Australian left doesn't really pay very close attention. On his Radio National program on September 12, Adams interviewed American writer David Brooks, who made passing reference to budget cuts the US armed forces had endured over the previous eight years. Although the cuts were a major issue in the Presidential election held less than a year earlier, Adams knew nothing about them. 'I find that extraordinary,' he said, without apparent embarrassment.

So it shouldn't be a huge surprise that Adams blames the US for sanctions against Iraq that are in fact United Nations sanctions (Ellis makes the same mistake, writing that 'a thousand Iraqi children die of starvation each month because of American policy'), or that he mocks President George W. Bush's missile shield plan because it wouldn't be able to halt an airliner attack it was never designed to halt. Adams is almost as bewildered as FitzSimons, who asked in June: 'Even if it did prove possible to shoot missiles out of the sky, as the Americans claim, just how does that prevent ships from rogue states sailing into any American port and letting loose?' It doesn't, Fitz. That's why it's called a 'missile shield'. It stops missiles. The thing you're thinking of – you know, the boat-stopping thing – is called 'the US Navy'.

'Now Bush demands justice,' Adams wrote as Operation Infinite Justice began. 'Not UN justice, only US justice'. The Australian left's lust for the UN is proportional to its loathing of the US. 'A responsible leader of this country would have advised George Bush to take this terrible crime to the United Nations for investigation', complained letter-writer Stephen Langford, ill-informed, of Paddington.

Could it be that bin Laden reads Australian newspapers? Seems so, because on November 3 he felt obliged to put matters straight: he hates the UN even more than he hates the US. In a speech broadcast on Al-Jazeera satellite television, Osama declared: 'Those who refer our tragedies today to the United Nations for solutions are hypocrites who are deceiving God, his prophet and the believers'. He's talking to you, Phil, you big God-deceiver! 'Are any of our tragedies not the making of the United Nations? Who issued the resolution for the division of Palestine in 1947 and surrendered the land of Islam to the Jews? It was the United Nations in its resolution in 1947.' So much for the UN's chances of brokering a deal between Binnie and Bush.

The left's confusion over the attacks turned incomprehensible once America outlined its response. FitzSimons cited the 'strong arguments' of American Muslim Tamim Ansary: 'We come now to the question of bombing Afghanistan back to the Stone Age. Trouble is, that's been done … Make the Afghans suffer? They're already suffering. Level their houses? Done. Turn their schools into piles of rubble? Done … New bombs would only stir the rubble of earlier bombs'. An Afghan woman, Makiz Ansari, told an anti-war rally in Sydney that 'warring against a poor country such as Afghanistan is futile … war should not be a war on Afghanistan, this isn't the poor country's fault'. The *Sydney Morning Herald*'s Margo Kingston railed about 'bombing the bejesus out of Afghanistan'.

What on earth were these people talking about? There was never any war against Afghanistan. Never planned to be, never was. It was a war against Osama bin Laden and the Taliban who harboured him, not Afghanistan. That's why, once the Taliban were routed, the schools – far from being turned into 'piles of rubble' – were quickly filled with girl students, for the first time in five years. With the Taliban gone, Afghanistan remains.

As I write this, seven weeks into the conflict, Afghanistan is looking better by the day, despite the warnings of FitzSimons ('a conventional attack on Afghanistan, with bombs and occupying ground troops and all the rest, is complete madness') Adams ('let us not share the madness') Kingston ('what will we do when the war begins, and millions more flee in terror?') and letter-writer John Brunton, completely wrong, of Sutherland: 'If George Bush attacks Afghanistan it is certain to unite the whole Muslim world against the US and its allies. It will be all Muslims against the US and its partners'.

A Knight Ridder report from post-attack Kabul seemed to answer most questions about indiscriminate US bombing: 'Residents were surprised at the depth of American intelligence. US aircraft fired laser-guided rockets at specific houses in crowded neighborhoods that residents were only vaguely aware contained Arab and Pakistani militants sympathetic to Osama … "We were amazed at the accuracy," said Mohammad Alem, a carpenter from the Qasabale-Kargere housing complex.'

In Australia, we were amazed at inaccuracy, specifically Kingston's. 'It's hard to find victory or exit strategies or any other sanity in what's happening', she 'wrote' a couple of weeks into the conflict. 'Innocent bodies pile up. Moral certainties dissolve. Regional tensions mount ... As predicted by everyone except the Yanks, it appears, it's supposed be [sic] a LONG war, requiring PATIENCE and INTELLIGENCE.'

And LOTS of CAPITAL LETTERS. Strangely, Kingston had earlier claimed to have watched Bush's September 20 speech to Congress, when he had said, very clearly: 'Americans should not expect one battle, but a lengthy campaign, unlike any other we have seen'. So where did Margo find these 'Yanks' who didn't predict a 'LONG war'? (Note to cadet journalists: voices in your head are not reliable sources.)

As for 'all Muslims turning against the US', well, it depended on which Muslim you spoke to. The thousands dancing in the streets of liberated Kabul looked happy enough, and were too busy burning *burqas* and playing soccer to bother 'fleeing in terror'. Boxer and leading Australian Muslim intellectual Anthony Mundine took the anti-US approach ('It's about fighting for God's laws, and America's brought it upon themselves [for] what they've done in the history of time') but quickly recanted, possibly when he discovered that his idol, Muhammad Ali, opposed the attacks: 'These radicals are doing things that God is against. Muslims do not believe in violence. If the culprits are Muslim, they have twisted the teachings of Islam. Whoever performed, or is behind, the terrorist attacks in the United States of America does not represent Islam.

God is not behind assassins. Anyone involved in this must pay for their evil'. In or out of the ring, Anthony Mundine isn't fit to carry Ali's spit bucket.

Another of Mundine's pronouncements – 'I really feel that it is not our problem' – was taken up by a number of his fellow deep-thinking Australian progressives. Fearful Margo Kingston wanted no part of the war: 'When I heard Howard say at his campaign launch that September 11 "was an attack on Australia as much as it was an attack on the United States" I felt less safe in the knowledge Howard would stay PM. To believe this is to be a fool'. Military strategist and historian FitzSimons believed Australia had no business becoming involved, and wrote: 'Have I missed something or is the whole thrust of our response so far been to write an absolutely blank cheque to the Americans?'

As usual, FitzSimons did miss something, or rather 22 things. That's how many Australians were killed in the WTC. Many other victims had deep connections to Australia. Peter Gyulavary moved to New York from Australia after marrying Jane, an American, but missed his homeland so much that he insisted – nationalist Fitzy will appreciate this – that their Orange County home be painted green and gold. At Peter's memorial service, Jane Gyulavary displayed an album full of images of Australia. 'I always knew,' she said of her late husband, 'that Australia would bring me something special and magical.' Former Sydneysider Craig Gibson shared Fitzy's love of sport and humour; he played for a soccer team in Manhattan named Barnestonworth United, after the fictional team in Michael Palin's *Ripping Yarns*.

Not our war, eh?

I suppose the war, such as it was in the days before America had commenced bombing, was nothing much to do with Tom Kaade, either. Kaade lives in South Bend, Indiana, hundreds of miles and a cultural light year away from New York City. His instant response to the WTC attack was to load his friends Ron and Wayne aboard his Dodge pickup truck and drive twelve hours straight to Ground Zero, where the trio loaded (and reloaded, and reloaded) the truck with ice and drinks to refresh rescue workers. 'Help yourself to a drink, sir,' Kaade called out to every cop, ambulance staffer or fireman who wandered past. At some stages they were giving away 640 bottles of water and soft drink every hour, while Kaade seethed in the cabin, looking at the smoke rising from the rescue site, quietly furious that there was nothing more he could do to help. Kaade wasn't much in the mood to apologise to anyone.

Nor should he have been. An apology made for something you haven't done represents a kind of death: a death of justice, or truth. There are deaths and there is Death; I would have preferred to have taken my chances in the World Trade Centre on September 11 than live in the soulless, unfeeling, inhuman void where the likes of Ellis, Adams, FitzSimons, and Kingston dwell. They place ideology above humanity. They seek to justify evil. They witness chaos, and see reason.

They would walk Manhattan streets that scream with suffering, and hear not a sound.

Blaming the Victim

Margaret Fitzherbert

On September 11 several thousand people in New York City became the initial victims of a violent criminal attack. We can assume that some – mercifully – died immediately. Others tried in vain to escape the danger. Some acknowledged that their fate was to die and tried to minimise harm to others. All were victims. But some victims of terrorism, it seems, are more deserving of our sympathy – or more 'innocent' – than others.

The world reeled in the days that followed the attacks, still coming to terms with the enormity of 'what' before it could deal with 'why'. But soon some discordant voices were heard. These were the writers and commentators who argued that America was responsible for the tragedy that befell it in New York and Washington, as a consequence of its own actions and its own history. It was also put that this was not any kind of attack on values or liberty. It was simply a retaliatory attack on America.

Margaret Fitzherbert has a BA (Hons) in politics from Monash University and a Grad Dip in Labour Law from the University of Melbourne. She has worked as an industrial advocate and is a former adviser to the Howard Government. Currently working as a communications specialist in the private sector, she has written widely about women and politics.

These arguments are as unsustainable as they are uncompassionate. I suspect that most newspaper readers discount them and move on. From time to time however it is useful to reflect on these kinds of knee-jerk comments and offer a countering view that responds to the fallacious arguments that have been made.

Did America bring the attacks on itself?

It was the American writer Susan Sontag who kicked off this theme in a short and jarring article that was published in the September 24 edition of the *New Yorker*. In her stinging three-paragraph piece, which drew widespread condemnation in the United States, Sontag memorably described the events of September 11 as 'an attack on the world's self-proclaimed superpower, undertaken as a consequence of specific American alliances and actions'. Australian writer Raimond Gaita had a similar view of America's self delusion and ignorance, describing 'the grotesque self-deception that appears to afflict many Americans and which enables them to believe that America was, before September 11, (as Edward Said put it) a sleeping giant, innocent of anything that might even partially explain (though of course not justify) why its government, but not its people, is hated in some parts of the world'.

Phillip Adams, writing in the *Australian* on 6 October, picked up the theme of the Americans bringing it on themselves and foolishly ignoring their own history:

'Let's by all means grieve together. But let's not be stupid together.' Susan Sontag gives good advice to her fellow Americans – and even better to Australians. Let us not share the madness with a nation that, instead of understanding its history, believes its own publicity. Confusing itself with the sanitised representations in Disney theme parks, the US fails to see that it has always been among the most violent nations on earth.

It's a damning message, and one devoid of empathy or compassion. It has parallels with recent Australian experience, where some have argued that individuals should not only feel sympathy, but should bear responsibility for the sins of the past – events that may have happened well before their birth.

As evidence Adams offered a long list of violent episodes in America's history. And after this long, sad list came the clincher: 'The US has to learn that its own worst enemy is the US'. It is not clear to me how events that are mainly internal to the US can have causal relevance to foreign powers. The most glaring omission, however, is that Adams's article does not include his response to the obvious question: does this history, which is undoubtedly violent, in any way justify the horrific terrorist attacks on America on September 11? Is an attack on thousands of civilians on US territory a reasonable reaction to their country's violent history? Even if it is somehow logical, in a schoolyard, tit-for-tat kind of way, is it right or just?

It is simply illogical to contend that it is somehow alright for a group of men to crash loaded passenger jets into New York's tallest buildings, because, over the preceding two centuries, America has had many violent episodes.

Neither should individual Americans simply expect that, because their nation has a violent history, they have in some way invited this attack against them – and should simply accept this.

It is akin to a court of law providing a jury with a list of previous charges against an accused person, just before the jury decides whether it was *justifiable* for that person to be the victim of an unprovoked and violent attack. To give a more specific parallel, and one with which most of the community and particularly the left would identify, it is just as irrelevant as a court of law seeking to examine the sexual history of a victim of sexual assault when considering the charge against her alleged assailant.

And why single out America? There are other nations that have violent histories. England is one. It was on the other side of the War of Independence, and it also had its own civil war. It too has a history of violent riots, some of it in the very recent past. Would this justify an attack on the City area of London? Is there an issue about *how* violent a nation needs to be, to invite this kind of external attack? Would Australia qualify?

In the days immediately after the attacks, many questioned the role of America's security agencies. Why hadn't this elaborate plot been detected? It's a fair enough question to ask. For others though, the question was more pointed. It was not just the professional security agencies that missed it; why didn't 'America' see it coming? America's shock was translated into a general failing by its governments and its people – another symptom of its smug arrogance. Peter Hartcher's thoughtful and detailed piece in the *Australian Financial Review* again pointed to a perceived ignorance of history: 'America's decade long holiday from history is over. It's a measure of just how complete that holiday was that so few foresaw its shattering end'.

It seems that not only did few Americans see it coming – not a lot of writers and columnists did either. There was no big rash of articles published right before September 11, explaining that obvious fate that was about to befall America. And why should there? It was a sudden criminal attack without recent parallel. On any view, it marked a new phase in international terrorism. And it is still unclear to me what the United States was supposed to actually *do* once it had heeded the warning. What reasonable step could or should have been taken to protect US citizens from the actions of the terrorists?

Like Phillip Adams, Hartcher included some examples of American arrogance and went on to contend that the terrorists' threats had been so clearly made that they should have been heeded:

> The orthodoxy that the world changed on
> September 11 out of a clear blue sky is almost
> perfectly wrong. The threats were explicit in their
> intent, advertising their anger, almost clamouring for
> attention, but undetected by Western ears attuned
> to the siren song of American triumphalism that
> rose insistently in the 1990s.

Hartcher explains that America's vulnerability was an almost ironic result of its status as the world's only surviving superpower. America's old rivals Russia and China had fallen by the wayside, their economies crumbling while the US stockmarket was powering ahead, carried along in part by the IT revolution. The Americans deluded themselves in thinking that they had '*earned*' this prosperity. While America wallowed in unearned prosperity, Osama bin Laden systematically used various platforms to publicise his terrorist intentions.

Bin Laden executed the bombings of a US–operated Saudi National Guard training centre in Riyadh in 1995 and of the US military residence in Dhahran in 1996, killing 24 Americans and two Indians. Two months after the Dhahran bombing, bin Laden issued and signed a formal *jihad* against the United States and Saudi Arabia. In 1998 he announced a terrorist partnership with two other terrorist organisations from Bangladesh and Pakistan, the World Islamic Front, which then announced that Muslims should kill Americans anywhere in the world – including civilians. Hartcher asks: 'With so many explicit threats and actual attacks from a known terrorist leader, was America justified in its shock when planes struck New York and Washington?'

The answer is 'yes' – it was reasonable that America was shocked. The attacks did not occur in a combat situation nor were they directed at military personnel. It was a very violent crime, in which thousands of people suddenly died. There was no warning to the civilian population – in fact, it appears that despite evidence of Osama bin Laden's desire to inflict harm on the US, there was no specific warning about what was planned for New York and Washington. At the end of the day, the World Trade Centre was knocked down by a paper cutter. That's pretty shocking.

It is quite different to the experience in the United Kingdom, where Irish terrorists have a long history of warning of terrorist attacks. In 2000 I was on the Tube in London when public transport authorities suddenly announced the immediate closure of two lines, including the one I was travelling on, in response to terrorist bomb threats. As we exited at the nearest station, the locals around me faced this threat with resignation and irritation rather than obvious fear. What was happening was routine. London has faced fairly regular bombing since World War II. There is arguably little shock value. Londoners are long acclimatised.

Those who defend the actions of the terrorists by characterising them as a reaction to American foreign policy, or as a response to a perception that the Americans have a violent history, are advocating a double-standard that seems to be based more on a personal dislike of America and its culture than on a rational assessment of what are reasonable standards of behaviour for nations. And that is a long way from the view that while individuals, groups and nations have rights, there are also obligations, one of which is to behave in a manner that is reasonable and respects the rights of others – whoever you are, and whatever your cause.

This was not an attack on 'values'

In the immediate aftermath of the terrorist attacks, US President George W. Bush made it clear that he considered the attacks to be an attack on 'American values'. In his address to the nation on the evening of September 11, the President stated that on that day America's 'way of life, and

our very freedom came under attack in a series of deliberate and deadly terrorist acts'. He returned to the theme of
values when he said that the United States would seek to
ensure that it remained the 'brightest beacon of freedom
and opportunity in the world'. Again it was Susan Sontag
who was one of the first to argue that the terrorist attacks
were not an attack on values. Sontag argues that America
has been attacked because of its foreign policy – or maybe
because of its history since settlement. But can these
actions be somehow detached from America's values?
Surely there is an inherent link?

The most devastating military or terrorist attacks are
those that are loaded with powerful symbolism as well as
physical power. This is because one of the distinctive features of terrorism is the specific intention by terrorists to
invoke fear amongst a civilian population. One way to do
this is unexpectedly to threaten someone's physical safety,
or that of someone close to him or her. Another way is to
undermine confidence in accepted modes of behaviour, or
to threaten an object or ideal or symbol that is held dear.

The attack on America had obvious symbolism. The
most brutal attacks were against the city that is an American icon – a city that had generated myth and legend for
a couple of hundred years before the attacks. The World
Trade Centre formerly stood at the heart of the financial
district in Manhattan. It was an audacious building that, for
many, symbolised the often aggressive might of the American economy, and globalisation in general. In attacking the
World Trade Centre, the terrorists attacked one of the most
visible signs of American capitalism on the thrusting New
York skyline.

It was also an attack on the freedom and liberty of many thousands of individuals – freedom and liberty as they are expressed in the most simple of ways. The freedom to go about your lawful business, without fear of violent attack. The freedom to work, and to be paid for your labour. The ability to travel freely within your own country. The freedom to walk into a shopping mall, window-shop for a while and then linger over a coffee. On September 11 it was these mundane expressions of individual freedom, which are familiar to all of us, that led many people to their deaths.

In the weeks immediately after the terrorist attacks it became obvious that this was an extremely carefully planned assault that had been plotted and slowly implemented over a long period of time. It was clearly intended to have maximum impact in terms of immediate casualties and injuries. But it was also intended to cause additional harm through a series of after-shocks that were mainly economic in nature. These after-shocks quickly travelled through the globalised economy and into individuals' homes and lives.

For all that Osama bin Laden has been dismissed as a backward, cave-dwelling proponent of fundamentalism, in truth he has a greater understanding of Western economies than the average Western citizen. Bin Laden is the son of a Saudi construction billionaire and formerly ran his own network of companies in the Sudan as well as organising financial support for several radical Islamic groups. There is credible evidence to suggest that he, or his associates, actually profited from the September 11 attacks by short selling targeted securities on the Tokyo Stock Exchange in the days before the attacks.

The September 11 attacks had an immediate and crippling effect on the viability of airlines, the travel industry and their associated industries. The insurance sector was hit hard. Thousands of people in America and beyond were affected by a deliberate attack on the free market system – the same free market system that provides their income, puts a roof over their heads and meals on their tables. It was a secondary attack on individuals, but it was also an attack on the values of the system in which they live, which have been explicitly condemned by Osama bin Laden and his associates.

On November 12, 2001, there were media reports that Osama bin Laden had justified the deaths of the victims of the terrorist attacks. His reported comments provide a neat counter to those who argue that the terrorist attacks were a predictable response to US foreign policy or the violence of American society, and have nothing to do with symbolism or values. It's also something to think about for those who depict the Americans as being smug and arrogant in their inability to predict these events – and criticise them for being shocked in the aftermath of the attacks.

Bin Laden justified the deaths of those who died in the World Trade Centre saying that they were 'not civilians' but were 'legitimate targets'. Bin Laden is alleged to have said:

> The towers were supposed to be filled with supporters of the economic powers of the United States, who are abusing the world. Those who talk

about civilians should change their stand and reconsider their position.

Part of the horror of the September 11 attacks is the realisation that terror and violence and death could so easily envelop people who were simply going about their morning routine like those in any other commercial centre. People just like us, in a place fairly similar to ours.

On the morning after the terrorist attacks my office was pretty quiet. There was not much conversation except for some stilted comments about what we all had seen on CNN very early that morning. We dissected the events in our offices. It was a backdrop that had a disturbing similarity to the place where thousands of people had suddenly and unexpectedly been murdered only a few hours before. My summing up of these events comes from one of my work colleagues, an American who was sharing an office with me on the morning of September 12: 'I know we haven't been perfect,' she said. 'I don't agree with all our foreign policy, and we've made mistakes.' She even listed a few examples for me before adding, 'But we didn't deserve this.'

Emails from the Edge

Miranda Devine

Two days after September 11, with people still trapped under the rubble of the World Trade Centre, *Sydney Morning Herald* reader Michael, from Newtown, wrote me this email: 'Eat shit and die Bush. You and your corrupt, manipulative family deserve everything you get. I don't want Australia to be like America. In Newtown we managed to get rid of KFC and McDonald's and Starbucks won't show its face and that's the way we like it'. Michael's email came from his workplace, a global telecommunications company whose largest client is the US.

At the time it seemed like a sick little aberration. But over the weeks it became clear that there were a lot of people, including the cream of the West's intellectual class, who felt just like Michael, but expressed it more elegantly.

A week after September 11, my editors sent me to New York. The fires still raged under the rubble downtown and black smoke still poured into the bright blue sky

---

Miranda Devine is a columnist for the Sydney Morning Herald *and* Sun-Herald. *She worked previously for Sydney's* Daily Telegraph, *the* Boston Herald, USA, *and the CSIRO. She has a Bachelor of Science in mathematics from Macquarie University and a Master of Science in journalism from Northwestern University, Chicago.*

above the financial district. If the breeze was right, the acrid stench of the fires could waft as far as the Upper East Side. There was another smell, too, richer, darker, more awful, that people didn't talk about, and which never seemed to travel much higher than West 11th street. People said the city was breathing the ashes of the dead.

Firefighters were being buried every day in the unfashionable suburbs, Queens, Brooklyn, Staten Island, and the newspapers were full of photos of their widows and children. Flowers and candles and pictures of Jesus and the Virgin Mary piled up around the small fire stations which are located about every eight blocks in Manhattan, some of which had lost more than half their men. Six blocks from Ground Zero, at Ivy's Bistro on Greenwich Street, firemen and construction workers used to take a break each afternoon from their grisly round-the-clock work sifting the rubble for human remains. They would sit at the gloomy bar and drink white wine with ice and talk about what they had seen, the fingers, the small bits of flesh, the intact human spine, shorn of all meat. They talked about it all in gruesome detail, as if to expunge the horror by sharing it. The smell was so bad at the place they called The Pit they had to wear Vaseline under their noses as they worked. They used to place each piece of humanity inside an individual body bag, retrieving its dignity, painstakingly connecting it back to the smiling faces on missing posters all over the city.

After a week, I returned to Australia, whose Prime Minister had been one of the first world leaders to pledge support for the US on September 11, for which he had been given a standing ovation in Congress, since he happened to be visiting Washington at the time of the attacks. Opinion polls showed that four out of five Australians supported his stand. But this attitude was not reflected in the opinion and letters pages of Australian newspapers. At home, my piled-up back issues were like a slap in the face. Here was the worst of anti-American thought, from home and abroad, displayed generously, as if it were reasonable and widely shared. Some of the emails from readers were just as bad. Missing was any understanding of the suffering, the resolve and the restraint so evident in the United States, from rescuers, the bereaved, politicians and ordinary citizens.

The ill-considered and intemperate comments of various well-known left-wing commentators are quoted elsewhere in this book. But their perspective had plenty of support in the letters pages.

Radwan Chahine, of Greenacre, wrote to the *Daily Telegraph*: 'It is with great hypocrisy that the US accuses others of being faceless cowards and terrorists. Is it not terrorism for thousands of innocent people to starve and die because of food and medical sanctions placed on them in Iraq?' Peter Aubrey, North Curl Curl: 'Is it possible that the acts of terrorism in the US are a protest against the very same thing many Australians are unhappy about capitalism gone mad?' Walter Bass, of Turramurra, wrote to the *Sydney Morning Herald*: 'It wouldn't take a genius to work out that if the US spent on food, clothing and economic aid for poorer countries (with no strings attached) the money it's spending on the huge army it is assembling, most of the terrorists in the world would soon disappear'. Russ Grigg, of Lorne: 'Being the most hated and largest terrorist organisation in the world, does this mean that not only will the Yanks have the proud distinction of starting the first war of the 21st century, but also be the first country in history to declare war upon itself?'

Like Michael from Newtown, these people were triumphant, gleeful even. Here at last was America's come-uppance. Hadn't they been warning for years that the end was nigh for the Great Satan, purveyor of globalism and inequity, which should have seen what was coming and which brought its misfortune on itself, the inevitable result of the haves having more than the have-nots? They couldn't wait to rub it in.

It became hard to differentiate between these sentiments and a message to the American people from the Taliban supreme leader, Mullah Mohammad Omar, delivered through the Pakistan-based news agency, the Afghan Islamic Press: 'Your government is perpetrating all sorts of atrocities in Muslim countries. Instead of supporting your government's policies you should urge your government to reconsider their wrong and cruel policies. The recent sad event in America was the result of these cruel policies and was meant to avenge this cruelty'. Columnists like John Pilger and Phillip Adams couldn't have said it better themselves.

How quickly they had hardened their hearts to the dead. In one firm alone in the World Trade Centre, Cantor Fitzgerald, 1,500 children lost a parent, in some cases their only parent, just one tragic fact among thousands that came from the evil perpetrated on September 11. But almost 4000 dead was nothing on a global scale, they said. When did anyone hold candlelight vigils for the dead babies of the Middle East?

Reader Victor von der Heyde's email to me was typical: 'Given that the US-led sanctions on Iraq kill between 4000 and 5000 persons (mainly children) PER MONTH, every month (UN figures), which is about 50,000 per year, why are you so concerned about 6000 dead in the US. The sanctions on Iraq have not weakened the power of Saddam Hussein. Where is your humanity? Do you only care for Americans?'

Elham Monavari wrote 'the US is hated because it imposes itself on everyone else', although later in his email he complained that the US 'did not do anything for years about Kosovo when Muslims were being slaughtered there'. No plaudits from Monavari for the US-led NATO intervention in Kosovo, which saved thousands of Muslims. 'I don't think that it's rocket science why America is hated,' he continued, 'and it shouldn't be too hard to move beyond Hollywood, McDonald's and Coca Cola to see that most of what they do to make their own lives better and protect their way of life is killing others around the world. Think of the Kyoto protocol.'

Another dissatisfied reader, Mark Cleaver, wrote in an email: 'You are clearly a misinformed snot-nosed brat. While I don't condone the attacks on the WTC and the Pentagon, they were no more an act of terrorism than the bombing of Nagasaki and Hiroshima … Even a bimbo like yourself should be able to see that America is far from innocent. They've had this coming for years. Can't you see why they are hated by so many people. Probably not, Pollyanna. Wake up and smell the blood'.

If you happened to feel outrage or grief for the victims of September 11, that was just a construct of your cultural insularity, according to those who live in the confusing world of moral relativism. 'Ms. Devine's claim that the suicide pilots could not be viewed as anything other than terrorists is simply misguided as it fails to assess them from their own cultural perspective,' wrote PhD student Lauchlan Mackinnon, of Erskineville, in a letter to the *Sydney Morning Herald*.

In another letter to the editor, Pat O'Shane, magistrate of Hunters Hill, complained about a profile of kamikaze pilot Mohamed Atta in the *Herald*. 'It does nothing to suggest he is/was a "terrorist".' Was there ever any question that the man who piloted a plane full of innocent civilians into an office building full of innocent civilians was a terrorist?

Right from the beginning, peace protesters and appeasers had been exhorting the US not to act rashly or lash out in anger, never noticing that for weeks President Bush and his team hadn't been dropping bombs but calmly gathering evidence, building their coalition and planning their offensive. At the University of Technology, the Free the Refugees coalition called an anti-war 'Day of Action' for September 29 with the motto: 'No to US War. No Australian troops or support. No to racist scapegoating. Defend democratic rights'.

Linda Rutter of Mayfield East wrote to the *Daily Telegraph* on September 25: 'The US does have an alternative to its apparent present course of action. It would take an incredible amount of courage and would be almost inhumanly humbling. They could do nothing'. Eugenia Mitsakis wrote in an email: 'John Howard not only has the physical behaviour of a puppet but I believe he is a puppet and I know he will not be around when the bodybags start piling up. An appeaser is one who feeds a crocodile hoping to tame it'.

There were dire warnings from experts about the impregnability of Afghanistan. It would be winter soon and our helicopters would fall out of the sky and our soldiers would freeze in the mountains and we'd have to wait until spring and what was the point? Better to give up and make friends with our enemies rather than suffer the same humiliating defeat as the Russians. Writing in the *Sydney Morning Herald* on September 28, decorated Brigadier Adrian D'Hage called for the US not to wage war against terrorists, but instead 'start a dialogue', build schools and hospitals, and invest in food, training and agriculture in 'these desperate communities'.

On October 7, after the first US attack on Taliban airfields in Kabul and Kandahar, reader Jock Webb emailed me: 'I suppose you will be cheering the launch of cruise missiles this morning. I am older than you and have seen a lot more of how these things work. If one innocent Afghani is dead today then the whole mission is a failure'. On October 28, Peter Woods, president of the NSW Local Government Association, used the opening address of the LGA's annual conference in Wollongong in November to launch an extraordinary attack on Australia's support of the US in the war against terrorism: 'Our sycophantic following of the US with its appalling human rights record and equally appalling foreign affairs policies makes us look pathetic,' he said. Americans 'can't expect to go around the world causing all this strife and the overbearing economic interventions and expect there is not going to be a reaction'.

It was hard to understand the depth of anti-American feeling displayed in a country that, in World War II, was being bombed by the Japanese and was only saved from a terrible fate by the Americans. The US also saved Europe from Hitler, defeated communism in the Soviet Union, saved Kuwait from Saddam Hussein and helped stop Milosevic's slaughter in the Balkans.

But in the world that exists beyond local government conferences and PhD theses, beyond Newtown and the opinion pages, there was a different Australia, inhabited by that 80 percent of the population who approved of the Government's support of the US. These were the councillors who walked out on Peter Woods's speech. These were the 11,000 Sydneysiders who lined up to sign condolence books for the people of New York and Washington, or to lay flowers outside the US consulate. These were the people who flew American flags from their houses in solidarity with our US allies, even when the other Australia sneered. 'Two days after the New York attack I bought an American flag and hung it outside our front door,' emailed Michael Arnold of Coogee. 'I thought they needed a bit of support. Yesterday morning we found it ripped down and the flag torn from its little pole, so there are some fairly vitriolic left-wing wankers out there. Needless to say, the flag has been re-erected – only this time higher up and out of reach without a long ladder!'

In the end, the marvel is not how wrong the 'left-wing wankers' are, or even how morally defective, but how, despite their disproportionate voice and their claims to lead opinion, so few people pay attention.

Terrorism and Poverty: Has the Left Proved its Case?

John Roskam

In the aftermath of September 11 many theories emerged to explain the motivation behind such terrorism in the United States. Western countries were suddenly plunged into a morass of self-examination and self-doubt. What was it about America that could have prompted such hatred? Were its values, its hegemony, or simply that it represented a way of life abhorrent to others to blame? In truth we will never know. It was a combination of many factors. Trying to seek a single, all-encompassing explanation is bound to fail. What explains the Holocaust, or the evil of Stalin, or Pol Pot? It is human to want to know and it is frustrating when we cannot.

Following the attacks many commentators considered that such explanations as could be discerned were likely to be found in political and religious factors, and in

John Roskam is the Executive Director of The Menzies Research Centre, a research organisation in Canberra. He is completing his PhD on Australia's political culture at the Centre for Public Policy at the University of Melbourne. He has previously worked in Australia and the UK with the private and non-government sectors in the areas of corporate social responsibility and sustainable development.

the fanaticism of individuals. However, such analysis was rejected by the left. The left located the cause of September 11 in the existence of poverty and the inequality of wealth in the world.

This essay evaluates the claim that terrorism and poverty are inextricably linked and it examines the consequences of such a statement. By connecting terrorism and poverty the left is not seeking to understand terrorism but rather to critique capitalism. Such an interpretation has gained currency because of its superficial attractiveness, which can be explained on a number of grounds.

First, it is a simple explanation. It makes understandable the cause of the horror. Poverty is something that the public in developed countries believe they know something about. Its effects are clear to see. For the largely secular West it is almost impossible to comprehend what sort of religious fanaticism would drive people to suicide and the murder of thousands. It explains not only the existence of terrorism but also why the terrorists struck at the United States.

Second, arguing that terrorism is caused by poverty is reassuring because it implies that if poverty can be overcome then terrorism can be eradicated. It provides a plan for action. Something can be done about it. But if the terrorism was caused by religious or political motives then it would far more difficult to combat.

The dominance of the West against which the attacks were aimed provides the means by which terrorism can be defeated. All that is required is a modification, be it large or small, to the economic system that has allowed poverty to be created. If we built the system, so the argument goes, then surely we can change it. This is the position of those who feel uneasy about globalisation and who feel that its consequences advantage some more than others. To change the current system is regarded as achievable, and perceived to be costless, or close to costless.

If, to make the world a fairer place, the Gross Domestic Product per person in the United States were to fall from what it is now, at around $60,000, to say $50,000, then that is a small price to pay. Americans will still be far better off than the people of Sudan, which has a Gross Domestic Product per person of little more than $1000. Such reasoning excludes any other causes for the existence of poverty beyond the current capitalist system. Also not considered is the actual mechanism whereby wealth around the world would be equalised. Reducing the growth of the American economy would be to risk further impoverishing many nations. There does not have to be a trade-off between capitalism and fairness. Developed countries do not have to become poorer for less developed countries to become wealthier.

Flowing from the belief that capitalism has to be made 'fairer' is the view that to do this there must be imposed upon it restrictions enforced by supra-governmental organisations. The solution to the situation, according to the left, is to take economic management out of the hands of democratically elected national governments and place in it the hands of an organisation that represents the full range of affected interests.

Third, advancing poverty as the cause of terrorism avoids the other possible causes of terrorism, which may offend the cultural relativism to which much of the left subscribes. For example, if it were thought that the motivation of the attacks was to defend a theocracy that oppresses women, the left would be caught in a contradiction: it would have to condemn the absence of equal rights, but would be reluctant to make judgements that implied that one value system was preferable to another.

Finally, the left's assessment of September 11 conforms to a worldview that holds that the global financial and trading system is immoral, selfish, and unsustainable. Not only does it perpetuate economic inequality, but it breeds violence. The implication of this is to deny the role of human choice, and to accept the historical inevitability of events. Most egregiously, it lays responsibility for the terrorism at the feet of capitalism itself.

Such a thesis on what occurred emerged soon after September 11. Only days after the attacks it was expressed in the Commonwealth Parliament.

In a condolence motion in the Senate on September 17 expressing sympathy for the victims, Greens Senator Bob Brown said, 'We will not survive a world of inequality, for inequality breeds enmity and enmity breeds hate'.

Such sentiments were not restricted to the most left-wing party in the Parliament. On the same day Senator Meg Lees, a former leader of the Australian Democrats, said that we 'must also look at reducing the root causes of terrorism: poverty, alienation, oppression, corruption and the hopelessness that is felt by so many families when they cannot support, even with basic food, their own'.

Senator Vicki Bourne, also of the Democrats, used James Wolfensohn, head of the World Bank, to support her comments that we 'now have to go back and look with a new sense of urgency at poverty and desperation around the world, at the disparity of wealth between rich countries ...'

At the beginning of the twenty-first century we have become accustomed to having our questions answered. In the fields of medicine and science almost every day a new discovery tells us a little bit more about ourselves and our universe. But the methods of the natural world have limited applicability when analysing human actions. We should be wary of those who seek to find a single explanation for complicated events. It is too easy to claim that inequality breeds enmity and enmity breeds hate and that this explains September 11. Even if this were true, such a formulation runs the risk that in explaining an action it is excused and the individual responsibility for it is lessened. Such a tendency is prevalent in more than the world of international affairs.

Each of the senators mentioned expressed horror at what happened, and each sought an explanation in an aspect of what they perceived to be the ills of globalisation. Neither Senator Lees nor Senator Bourne identified religion as a possible motivation behind the attacks in their speeches. Senator Bourne went on to say that there was a lesson 'for all of us' in that those societies that crush dissent and lack tolerance breed fanatics. She made no mention of the United States being a country where dissent and tolerance positively flourish.

The most obvious example of how evidence is distorted comes simply by considering what is known of the circumstances of those who committed the attacks on America. They were not poverty stricken. Their deeds were not performed with the aim of establishing that economic system that has been the most successful at improving standards of living: Western capitalism. Just the opposite. Terrorism is violence committed as a calculated political act. It is often utilised by those from the middle class. Seldom is its aim to change economic conditions. Nationalism and the politics of identity and religion can be regarded as the stimulus to terrorism, not poverty. In his speech to the Senate, Brown spoke about the 'true goal of globalisation in terms of power must be one person, one vote, one value'. Terrorism is the absolute abrogation of that belief.

Certainly economics cannot entirely be separated from, for example, a desire for national self-determination. Nor can it be denied that those in poverty, if they practice terrorism, have more to gain economically, and less to lose. Those in poverty are less likely to have had their perspective on the world broadened by education. A lack of education may make individuals more susceptible to indoctrination, as was implied by Senator Bourne, but it may not. Totalitarianism gained root in Europe in the twentieth century within the most educated societies in the world. It is far too simple to claim a 'root cause' of terrorism is poverty.

A relationship between terrorism and poverty fits the materialist analysis of the left. The left has notoriously found it difficult to assimilate nationalism or religion into its account of human motivation. If human actions are determined by economic conditions, nationalism or religion or other motivations cannot be accommodated.

Aspects of the left's theories of economics, colonialism, and international relations are utilised to make the connection between poverty and the attacks in America. As the left would have it, the United States, and most, if not all Western economies have exploited the resources and the populations of less developed countries. The West has grown rich on the basis of that exploitation. Western countries as colonial powers exploited their colonies. The stain of colonialism is such that it will take generations for the exploited countries to recover and this explains the dire state that so many are in. Now in a postcolonial age the West achieves the same ends, not directly as in the past, but indirectly through the manipulation of the financial system and the operations of its multinational corporations. The result of this is to leave the people of the exploited countries impoverished. Those people are alienated and terrorism is their means of expression. It is the only way that their voice can be heard.

All of the above as a basic exposition would be well known to anyone vaguely familiar with Marxian theory. That the incidence of poverty is lowest in countries with the most highly developed capitalist economies is ignored. So is the fact that many former colonies have escaped economic destitution. 'Corruption', listed by Senator Lees as one of the 'root causes' of terrorism is rife, not in developed, capitalist countries, but in those countries that reject capitalism.

We should be careful not to impose on the past a framework of understanding that satisfies an ideological predisposition but that is not based on evidence. It is natural for us to attempt to make sense of events and to seek meaning in history. But from our analysis we should be careful not to conclude that events are inevitable. Human history is not the result of unalterable forces – whether those forces be economic, geographic, religious or something else. British philosopher Michael Oakeshott takes this view further. He argues that the past has no clear unity, that it has no pattern or purpose, and that it can't be used to support any practical conclusions. Such a position is at odds with that of the left, which sees in history an inextricable advance towards the collapse of the capitalist system. It is also provides no support to the right, who seek to find 'the end of history' in the fall of the Berlin Wall and the collapse of communism. The point of Oakeshott's comment is to emphasise the role of the free play of individual choices and freedoms in history. Belief in the impersonal forces of history depersonalises our history. It also leaves no incentive for us to change our circumstances if it is thought that what occurs is preordained.

Those who committed the atrocities in the United States made a conscious decision and bear responsibility for their actions. If we appreciate this we are in a far better position to deal with terrorism than if we simply ascribe poverty as its cause.

In the 1940s the economist Joseph Schumpeter noted the atmosphere of hostility to capitalism prevalent at the time. He said that condemnation of capitalism and all its works was almost a requirement of 'the etiquette of discussion'. The 'educated' hastened to conform to this attitude critical of capitalism, and any other attitude was regarded as not only foolish but anti-social and looked upon as an indication of 'immoral servitude'. Isiah Berlin, writing at around the same time, noted that collectivist solutions were considered altruistic while individualistic solutions were considered selfish.

At the beginning of the twenty-first century the left's position on capitalism has become more sophisticated. But the feigned moral superiority of opponents of capitalism over its defenders remains. In the face of the evidence of the successes of capitalism it is more difficult simply to condemn it; so, instead, the left attacks its perceived outcomes: inequality and poverty. Those who argue a position contrary to the left are placed in the invidious position of being seen to defend the indefensible, inequality and poverty. It is a difficult argument to make that free and open markets and liberal democratic institutions are the things that will help overcome these ills. A consequence of the left's position is to prevent the use of precisely those mechanisms that are most likely to help alleviate poverty. A free enterprise system that provides for the initiative of people to be rewarded is far preferable to any state-run alternative.

The tragedy of the left's interpretation of terrorism and poverty is that it blames the victim and gives the terrorists legitimacy. It is an interpretation that does not stand scrutiny. It merely conforms to the left's own preconceptions. However, the fact that it continues to be repeated demonstrates that it cannot be assumed that the idea of liberal democratic capitalism has triumphed against its adversaries. If there any lessons from September 11 this must surely be one of them.

Affinity Group: The Student Left, S11, and September 11

Matthew Thompson

Monkey was rabid, his filthy cluster of letters peerless in a year of hate mail. As a student at the University of Newcastle, Monkey took exception to his union fees filling the coffers of a 'gang of left-wing fuckwits'. *Opus*, the student magazine I co-edited in 2000, and which Monkey likened to *Pravda*, encapsulated all that he considered to be wrong with student politics. 'The way you arseholes jump on the bandwagon sickens me,' he wrote, spitting at the magazine's traditional fare of radical politics, yobbo jokes, and avant-garde art. 'I fucking hate Robert Mapplethorpe,' wrote Monkey after we published an analysis of the gender performance inherent in the notorious photographer's work. 'It's just a pity he didn't piss off and die sooner.'

'Easy to whinge if you never submit anything,' I emailed back. 'If more contributors are left-wing, then that's what mainly gets printed. It's no conspiracy.

Matthew Thompson was born in Oregon, USA, and now lives in Sydney. Educated at the University of Newcastle, he is the recipient of numerous writing and academic awards. His working life has ranged from mining and heavy industry to performing with an avant-garde theatre collective, the Institute of Amateur Surgery.

Write whatever you like.'

'I'm not a writer, you smug shit,' he replied.

The other half of my time was spent in email battles with left-wing critics. My co-editor and I had let the side down with the inclusiveness of our editorial policy. 'Free speech,' I was informed by Veronica, a prominent student activist, 'exists only when the marginalised are not intimidated into silence.'

'But we publish anyone. The only criteria's writing quality, and if it's no good I either give it back with a few pointers, or I fix it up myself'.

'Publishing just anyone is not free speech,' she replied. 'It precludes free speech. How can a woman or a gay person have the courage to express themselves if a magazine contains other material that invalidates their experience?'

'You'd be amazed', I said. 'Some even write stuff that might offend other women or gays or even gay women.'

'They're forced to,' said Veronica. 'Their only chance to speak is within the right-wing dictates of your so-called freedom of speech. The marginalisation of minority groups through sexism, racism, and homophobia is the basis of the mainstream press. That's why it's so important that the independent media, of which a key component is the student press, acts with complete left-wing solidarity'.

Editing a university magazine was never as simple as I wanted it to be. Throughout the year, my main concern was to present the contributions in as intellectually and aesthetically satisfying a manner as possible, yet from March to December mail flooded in accusing my co-editor and me of irresponsibility in our *laissez-faire* attitude to political content. Monkey, Veronica, and their many respective fellow-travellers raged at us for not being either inclusive or exclusive enough. The response of Monkey's team was basically, bugger it, give us our money back, while Veronica's was, hey, you're not doing enough to ensure that the Monkeys die out.

The trouble is, Monkeys abound, and they keep doing what they're not supposed to – believing in free speech and personal responsibility; voting conservative if they're so inclined; and feeling an affinity for the United States. When the nightmare happened on September 11, the student left was angry and confused: angry because the United States received so much sympathy, and confused because religious extremists had stolen their thunder. Just as it embarrassed them when Pauline Hanson led the charge against globalisation with greater impact than they ever managed, so too it embarrassed them when misogynist Muslim-supremacists outdid them in hating America by physically obliterating the Twin Towers of American economic might, and raining death on the United States' military command centre. Without delay the student papers and online discussion groups filled with anti-American vitriol.

From the National Young Writers Festival e-list:

> Although as a pacifist I regret any loss of innocent life in conflict, I am also sick of the hand-wringing about the terrorist attacks in the USA … What goes around comes around. Fuck the USA.

From *Opus*:

America will not take the opportunity to turn this
crisis into a kinder world [sic]; they will only
become more cruel and self-righteous ... we would
be deafened by the roar of silence if we honoured
every human being that dies every day at the hands
of American greed.

From *Vertigo* (student magazine of the University of
Technology, Sydney):

The USA are doing their best to create an evil
empire more global and more determined and more
dangerous than the Soviets ever were.

As always, everyone quoted or re-printed John Pilger,
who was amazed by 'how patient the oppressed have
been'. Clearly, someone should have blown up the United
States years ago. Of course, it would be unreasonable for
the United States to take military action against her attackers, and in a bold diplomatic move Newcastle University's
student union passed a motion to that effect. As
announced in *Opus*, 'The position ... has been declared to
the university, the media and all relevant consulates'.

If the anti-American rhetoric of the student left
seems reminiscent of terrorist groups, so do its methods.
Talk, of course, is cheap, but while not every politically
erect Environmental Science, or Communications (Event
Management) undergraduate is about to emulate the
Baader-Meinhof Gang, or join al-Qaeda, the student

left does more than talk. Functioning as nurseries for underground radicalism, the student unions provide money, training, and moral support to those who want to topple Western liberal democracy in favour of a new society where the obligations of law are overruled by a 'parliament of the streets', and where the ignorant many are re-educated to share the violent prejudices of the ideologically pure.

Back in 2000, when I was arguing with Monkey and Veronica, my colleagues were preparing for their own September 11. Thrilled to bits by the mayhem in Seattle that scuttled the World Economic Forum the previous November, Team Veronica was preparing to launch its own Battle of Seattle at the World Economic Forum's Asia Pacific Summit planned for the Crown Casino at Melbourne.

One winter evening I attended an S11 information session at Newcastle's council-subsidised Octapod activist centre. After donating to get in and donating for a cup of *chai*, I browsed through anti-McDonald's pamphlets, then picked my way through the twenty or so hipsters draped around the lounges, settled into a beanbag, and waited while the Octapod crew fiddled with their donated video projector. The crowd was the same as at every other Novocastrian counter-cultural gathering. Some were my colleagues on the student council; a few were prior Opus editors; others hailed from the various pro-hemp and wilderness committees, while the hippest of the hip were the grant-applicants behind the annual National Young Writers Festival.

The guest of honour was Amy, a woman in her early twenties from the activist heartlands of North America.

Touring with a clutch of Battle of Seattle videos, she inspired and recruited activists from Melbourne to Brisbane with tales of life in the front line of the people's war against the United States of America. Timmy, Amy's young assistant, was all weary passion and sad grins as he warmed us up with a speech about the United States's institutionalising its war against the underprivileged in 1944 when it called the world's economic elite to Bretton Woods, New Hampshire, for a meeting establishing the International Monetary Fund, the World Bank, and the International Trade Organisation. With the ground rules and regulatory bodies of globalisation in place, explained Timmy, and with Europe and Asia devastated by World War II, the United States set about its planetary plunder, its heartless and unceasing transfer of wealth from the poor to the rich. But as Timmy delivered his introduction to the crisis, the audience of slacker decadents, a gallery of henna and tie-dye, semi-cut hair and multi-pierced eyebrows, set their eyes on Amy.

Perhaps because discussions of American malevolence are par for the course at politically progressive functions, actual Americans are rare. For youth on the breadline, the Podsters are remarkably well travelled — someone's always in Guatemala or Laos, and often there's a funky Brazilian or Italian visiting — but Americans remain exotic. Amy was Canadian, but even so, her aura of clarity, her clear, trusting eyes, and her simple attire of jeans, sweater and sneakers were spellbinding. When Timmy shut up and the projector problems were overcome, Amy spoke of how great and terrible Seattle had been. Great in its showcasing of the people's unity and resourcefulness, and terrible in the naked brutality of American capitalism. Unfortunately Amy had missed the Battle, but her friends had been there, risking everything to capture footage of the day that all those activists, each representing 'millions of the world's poor', said, 'No more!'

For an hour we watched police in full body armour bludgeoning pathways through 40,000 protestors. A bowl of communal popcorn wobbled in the air before me, passed down by the student union's Education Officer, Melinda, muttering with horror and disgust at the spectacle of clubs, rubber bullets, tear gas and water cannon used in defiance of the People's wishes that the Forum not meet. Yet there were occasions for laughter and smiles. In sound-bites interspersed throughout the combat footage, the creativity, hope, love, and peaceful bravery of the masses shone through. Some of our comrades dressed as turtles, others in balaclavas and jackboots. We thrilled to the sight of Starbucks and Nike outlets smashed and spray-painted; 'FUCK THE WTO', 'FUCK CAPITALISM', and fuck a host of other things tagged in dashing red across Seattle's trashed central business district.

When the lights came back on, Amy smiled and held her hands to pray. She spoke of how the United States debased and corrupted life on Earth: genetically modified food; the relentless privatisation of utilities; trans-national corporations paying lower wages in developing countries; the patenting of DNA – all malevolent expressions of the American ideology. Plunder without conscience. In Canada, Amy told us, the government is being forced by the World Trade Organisation to privatise the glaciers. As the profit-driven deforestation of the planet accelerates, exacerbating salination and global warming, water will become the oil of the twenty-first century. Liquid power. And while the wretched masses of a withering planet slowly die, the American super-companies will dollop-out Canadian Pure at sky-high prices. I felt a hand on my shoulder. 'Fucking bastards, hey,' said Shane, one of *Opus*'s regular contributors, spitting flecks of popcorn.

You can't, however, just fling yourself against a super-power. Countless hours of planning and hard work made the Battle of Seattle such a success, but now, said Amy, they're alert to the popular resistance, so it's vital that all operations be meticulously organised. Experience shows that the police are likely to make pre-emptive raids on activist centres, hunting names, and hoping to break the chain of command. To defend ourselves against their intelligence units Amy recommended the formation of 'affinity groups' – small cells of committed activists who know and trust each other. Each affinity group, said Amy, must act independently, but in unison with the others. The forces of the state are weakest when we operate under shared values, but without central command. This model of action also reflects our democratic values, she said, and confuses those who think in terms of hierarchy.

Amy's conspiratorial inclusiveness brought the audience forward on their lounges. They revelled in the detail of revolution – in the manual of attack. 'How will the groups work together if they don't know each other?' asked a girl trapped in the hierarchical paradigm.

'There'll be marshals on the day', said Amy, 'who'll be in radio contact with each other so that if we need reinforcements somewhere, like if the police breach our lines, then they can direct more groups to that point. You won't know who they are before the day, but they'll have whistles and be highly visible.'

'But how will we know where we're supposed to be?'

'The S11 website will be online next week,' said Amy, 'with an e-list so the affinity groups can talk to each other.'

Timmy, who had no doubt climbed this arc of radical arousal with Amy at a dozen or so of the eastern seaboard's hang-out zones for the politically hip, straddled his chair, beaming.

Back at the headquarters of the Newcastle University Students' Association (NUSA), as the union is called, the student representatives buzzed with plans for affinity groups. With Melinda anticipating scores of justice-loving undergraduates signing on to 'Shut Down the World Economic Forum!', $5,000 and all of the union's media facilities were put at her disposal. Posters advertising the free trip to Melbourne were slapped all over campus; I wrote S11 articles for *Opus*, and no occasion was missed to spread the word. Spurning the usual dry rhetoric of anti-capitalist critiques, Melinda made a lively appeal to students to climb aboard. In her monthly *Opus* report, our Education Officer wrote:

> [I]magine how we could really get our digestive juices flowing if we all teamed up in September to bring the system down!!!!!! Yeah!!!!!! Excited? You should be – because it's all going to happen on one fantastic date – September 11.

Twelve of the university's 16,000 students accepted the challenge, of whom eleven were either union representatives or their friends. The twelfth was Jim, a grizzled mature-age student with a grudge against authority, sneered at in private by the rest of the NUSA affinity group for having 'regressive tendencies' (being a cantankerous old fart), but publicly lionised after being thwacked in the head by police.

With the exception of Jim, Melinda's Dozen came back changed; they drank heavily, joked together with impenetrably grim humour, seemed estranged from those who had stayed home, and often just wandered the campus with a thousand yard stare. In many cases their academic performance sank even lower – all they could concentrate on was the next time they could get back in the shit. Their perceptions of acceptable conduct diverged from the mainstream, and all criticism of their behaviour in Melbourne as violent, destructive and intimidating was dismissed as naïve and the product of media misrepresentation.

In 'S11 Diary' (the condition of the union's $5,000 contribution being that someone write a what-we-did-in-Melbourne piece for *Opus*), Lisa, the chain-smoking, anti-multinational ('Rollies don't feel so corporate, you know?') Communications student approaching a decade in student union activism, set the record straight: 'I didn't see a single violent protestor in the entire three days … The only violence I saw was from the police'.

While editing 'S11 Diary' I remembered Monkey and his *Pravda*-slurs, particularly when I tried to reconcile Lisa's comments on the violence with her brief mention of then-West Australian Premier Richard Court's S11 misadventure. Court's chauffeur had attempted to drive into the casino complex, whereupon the car was engulfed by protestors who spent an hour stomping on the roof, smashing panels and trying to rip it apart. '[H]e gets a bit stuck in the crowd,' wrote Lisa. 'Dumb Arse!'

It's a sad feeling to lose faith in an organisation while holding a position within it. Although I still found Mapplethorpe's *Self Portrait (with Bullwhip)* 1978 an arresting photograph, the emotional logic behind Monkey's rants won me over. Voting is optional in the student elections, and of the university's many thousands of students a startlingly large majority exercise their right not to vote (80 people voted Melinda in as Co-President in 2001), yet there is no choice of whether or not to become a financial member. The union's annual takings from membership fees are around $700,000.

There is a Mission Statement committing the union to facilitate a 'climate conducive to excellence in academic performance and personal development', and there is also a Constitution, of which one objective is 'not to directly or indirectly support or condemn any political or religious creed or organisation excepting insofar as shall be necessary to achieve the objectives of the Students' Association', but these are totally disregarded by student 'leaders' who spend thousands vilifying Americans, conservatives, and Western civilisation while simultaneously denouncing intolerance; who preach non-violence while revelling in anarchist thuggery; and who call for openness and tolerance while hating the very idea of free speech.

Appendix

Appendix: Blaming Ourselves

'Far from being the terrorists of the world, the Islamic peoples have been its victims – that is, the victims of American fundamentalism, whose power, in all its forms, military, strategic and economic, is the greatest source of terrorism on earth'. (John Pilger, *New Statesman*, September 13)

'As racial and religious tensions threaten to escalate into world war, the government's failure to calm them during the Tampa crisis – and even to inflame them now – is scandalous'. (Margo Kingston, the *Sydney Morning Herald* 'Webdiary', September 13)

'I disagree with the Prime Minister's comments. I think we need to take a stand back, have a look at this and the repercussions that Australia may face because of it. You see, the problem with terrorism – it won't just stop at America and Australia will be a target, surely enough Australia will be a target for it. Look at the policies of America. Look at the fact that America has had sanctions on the Middle East countries for some time. America has been imposing their own viewpoints on to other countries, which I don't believe is the right thing to do. Through lack of medical supplies a lot of these people in these countries are starving. They don't have the medical supplies, and it's only through retaliation.

'As I've said for many years here in Australia, don't impose other people's views and cultures on to our own people here, because we are retaliating ourselves. The people are doing the same in their own countries. They don't want the Western way of life. They want their own way of living, their own culture. Let them have it. I think the whole push globally for this globalisation push is the reason behind this. A lot of people are retaliating because they don't want globalisation. They don't want capitalism'. (Pauline Hanson, Radio 6PR, September 17)

'We have all been saddened and horrified at the events in the US last week. Many of us are now extremely worried about the talk of war and vengeance on the yet unidentified enemy, and the escalation of violence that may occur if bombing of towns and cities in targeted countries occurs. If you would like to stand up and be counted and send a message to our civic leaders and fellow Australians that indiscriminate violence against 'suspects' will not be OK, that the targeting of Muslims, Arabs, Afghanis or other people of a certain ethnicity, as undesirable, is not OK, or if you just want to be with others who are sad, worried and concerned about war and justice ...'(National Tertiary Education Union invitation to a Vigil for Justice and Peace, September 18)

'A Webdiary debate is unfolding on the causes of the catastrophe, and whether the United States must take some responsibility for it. This is a bitter and highly ideological debate, but one which, with good will, could inform us all'. (Margo Kingston, the *Sydney Morning Herald* 'Web-diary', September 18)

'The children hold hands as they walk into the assembly hall. The children sing 'Advance Australia Fair'. But they do not say any prayer, and the name of God is not invoked. The children at this school are not chanting verses of the Koran, or the Catholic catechism. They are not being told that theirs is the one true faith, or that they are God's chosen people. They are not being taught that they are better or different from other people because of what they believe. They are simply being told: be kind to one another. This is what last week's tragedy is about, surely? About what we teach the children? The men who made missiles out of aeroplanes were once some mothers' little boys … All written religions have some terrible passages. Christians, in general, appear more able to ignore the bad bits than people of some other religions … I do not think schools that teach religion should be publicly funded … Be kind to one another. Little children can understand that. Maybe, without invoking a god to tell us whom we should hate, we could all be kinder to one another'. (Pamela Bone, the *Age*, September 19)

'A lot of lies told in the last two weeks have hurt the things we believe in, or believed in once, and they should, per-haps, be listed:

     ★ That the attack on the World Trade Centre was the 'worst terrorist act in history'. Not by a long chalk. The firebombing of Dresden killed 135,000 people, the atomic bombing of Hiroshima 120,000 people, and at Nagasaki

80,000 people. None of these were military targets and their fiery ruin, by the British and the Americans, was terrorism.

* That the young hijackers were 'cowards who strike and run away'. No, they were very brave and they did not run away. They eagerly died for their cause at the point of impact over New York.

* That the terrorist attack was 'an act of madness'. It was not. It achieved a sane end, a real truce in Israel, and it powerfully publicised the daily suffering of the Third World under the unfeeling market capitalism of the First World'. (Bob Ellis, *Canberra Times*, September 25)

'Hello. We are sorry. We are desperately sorry that the world has now moved to the point where it is on the edge of an abyss from which there can be no return. We accept that such hate as drove the planes into the World Trade Centre towers can only have come from incredible suffering, and we are desperately sorry for that suffering, even if we are yet to come to grips with its specific cause'. (Peter FitzSimons, *Sydney Morning Herald*, September 25)

'The US has to learn that its worst enemy is the US'. (Phillip Adams, the *Australian*, October 6)

'When I look at my baby's face and face my fear, it is not the caves of Afghanistan that spring to mind, but the buildings of Canberra and the spectre of another three years in which Australia is encouraged, boatload by boatload, to turn away from its decency and honour'. (Joanna Murray-Smith, *Sydney Morning Herald*, October 30)

'The current and ongoing role of the US in the global South makes it morally impossible to line up with. Palestine and Iraq are the two causes which serve as the pretext for bin Laden's activities, yet the more serious crime has been the US government's active and zealous enforcement of the IMF/World Bank Structural Adjustment Programs and the WTO provisions which allow for the transfer of wealth from South to North. The human cost of this process in unnecessary suffering and cultural destruction over the last twenty years dwarfs anything thrown up by the fascism, Nazism, Stalinism or first-wave colonialism in the rest of the twentieth century'. (Guy Rundle, *Arena Magazine*, October-November)

'*Hell in the Pacific*, ABC, 9.30 pm: I watched two episodes of this series in a row and, by the end of it, I was washed out emotionally. It's not the death toll – in the end those numbers are just that, numbers. It's not the symmetry in watching last week's episode of the US government rounding up any citizens with a Japanese background and assuming they were the enemy, while today a new government does almost the same thing with Arab-Americans'. (Bernard Zuel, *Sydney Morning Herald*, December 10)

'After the recent great clouds of propaganda and the fierce demonising of our so-called enemies, and seeing as it's Christmas, I wonder – can we love them, perhaps even briefly.

I think we must try to and I know we can, but where it can't be done or won't be done, may we at least refrain from hating them so morbidly, as Lao Tzu has suggested?

Can we lay off a bit? Mercy, forgiveness, compassion. These are great treasures. If you don't use them you lose them. Sooner or later we all need to give and receive these precious gifts. Might we, can we, find a place in our heart for the humanity of Osama bin Laden and those others? On Christmas Day can we consider their suffering, their children and the possibility that they too have their goodness? It is a family day, and Osama is our relative'. (Michael Leunig, the *Age*, December 24)

'I was very interested, after the events of September 11, how that noble, American, patriotic-speak immediately swung in, and people could put their hands on their hearts and sing noble songs and say noble things, which I found utterly chilling … Terrorists, whatever: I was appalled when they were described as "terrible cowards". I thought they were incredibly brave, actually. They might have been totally misguided and clearly extremely dangerous, but they were not cowards. They were brave and I think that we have to use, as novelists, our imaginations, to understand that this is a form of humanity, extreme and strange though it may be.' (Marion Halligan, *7.30 Report*, ABC, January 4, 2002)

'It's not good enough for America to say, "These people are not like us. These people are fanatics." We had that in Australia with the story of the people being thrown overboard: "They're not like us, therefore they throw their children overboard instead of sending them to Geelong Grammar. Therefore, you know, we don't have to worry about such people." That's an inadequate way to deal with the problem.' (Thomas Keneally, *7.30 Report*, ABC, January 4, 2002)

'Repeated headlines about a "Clash of Civilisations" provokes the thought that they should read the "Clash of Barbarianisms". Yet that is as crude as George Bush's asserting the goodness of his America, or the Ayatollah Khomeini's condemnation of the US as "The Great Satan". The best of US civilisation is represented by Mark Twain and W.E.B. du Bois, whom both Bush and Osama bin Laden would regard as devilish.' (Humphrey McQueen, *Sydney Morning Herald*, January 14, 2002)

'Imran Khan – Islam and America, SBS, 8pm: Having had a steady diet of Uncle Sam's propaganda since the September 11 attacks, the idea of a prominent Muslim discussing Islam is somewhat refreshing. As tragic as the events were, Sheriff Dubya's "We're gonna smoke 'em out" mantra is now getting just a tad tedious.' (Henry Everingham, *Sydney Morning Herald*, January 14, 2002)

Selections from the Letters pages of the *Sydney Morning Herald* and the *Australian*:
    'Cuba, Chile, Vietnam, Nicaragua, New York. What goes around comes around'. (September 14)
    'Any violence against mad terrorists must be measured and limited to protect ourselves. It must be complemented by a commitment to redressing economic and political inequities – the fuel for terrorism. Many people considered the WTO to be the expression of that inequity, despite the denials mainly from the privileged First World. We must avoid, as far as it is humanly possible,

given our grief and anger, to be driven by revenge'. (September 14)

'Terrorism against the US will tragically continue until the US can use its might to bring fairer outcomes to those who have been oppressed and ravaged by US foreign policy. The acts of terrorism are terrible evidence that US foreign policy in the Middle East has failed'. (September 14)

'Why did some Palestinians cheer? It is not because many Americans died but rather that the hypocritical, mighty tormentor has been humbled. And nothing gladdens the heart of the downtrodden than the sight of a fallen Colossus'. (September 14)

'Despite the horror at the loss of human life on September 11, what Phillip Adams said struck a chord with many. Bullies tend to bring out salutary responses'. (December 12)

'It would be tempting to nominate Osama bin Laden for an Oscar. The category could only be supporting actor, though. The person who masterminded the successful attacks on the World Trade Centre and the Pentagon is not someone who would allow videos of his briefings to be made so that they could be left lying around for Americans to find. There is a deeply disturbing aspect to this video farce. And can it really mean that they had even less than that bodgie video to go on before starting to destroy a country? This would be a war crime of the highest order, a crime against humanity next to which the events in New York of September 11 would fade into the background'. (December 19)

Selections from letters to Margo Kingston's 'Webdiary' (*www.smh.com.au/news/webdiary/*):

'It was an elegant plan. Use the power of the products of capitalism against itself. I wondered about what violence had preceded these unspeakable acts and what violence would follow. After all the Brits and the Yanks have been bombing Iraq for the last 10 years'. (September 12)

'I was down in the carpark putting the shopping into the boot and two young men of Middle Eastern appearance were walking towards their car and I had to resist the urge to stare and so I turned away. Twenty four hours of unrelenting American news reports and I feel compelled to turn away from my fellow citizens. What is happening Margo?' (September 13)

'The phrase global war is being tossed around. The term "the new war" is also being said. New is fine in the unfamiliar sense – but certainly not in the improved sense. Dubbya's [sic] speech labelling this the first war of the new century is more madness. Coz it doesn't count unless America is involved. In one sentence he said he was a loving man, but had a job to do. This is from the former Governor who has a record in overseeing executions on death row. Despite not having the greatest respect for Bill Clinton I keep wishing he was in charge'. (September 17)

'It is REALLY about the frustrated resentment of the 80% and more of the global population who suffer from Western globalism throughout the third world, and just about anyone else who has grown fed up with Global Capital's peculiar notion that the entire earth and it's [sic] population exist as some sort of playground for economic rationalist Big Business. Rob enough people for long enough of hope for ANY sort of future and eventually a reaction must occur. If you have nothing left to live for, you have nothing left to lose'. (September 17)

'Unless we can honestly address and try to remedy the issues of unfairness and abuse in world affairs, we are doomed to go all the way with competition whose end-points are mayhem and war'. (September 17)

'In the face of a huge disaster many people take a sentimental/emotional prejudiced tribal position and dig in to defend it. By force if necessary! This position allows no ambiguity, no shades of grey, no evolution as circumstances and knowledge change. This kind of primitive response is different only in degree to that of those who perpetrated the violence in the US. The chickens will surely come home to roost here too. We have destroyed much of our educational and cultural infrastructure. We have destroyed much of our social capital. We are now being manipulated by a Prime Minister and Cabinet in the most callous way. When we as a country need most to be thoughtful and considered, working together to address very complex issues, we cant [sic] do it. Why? Because contrary to the economic rationalist point of view, it bloody well does matter if you rape our social capital, cause when the chips are down that's what holds our society together. The disintegration of our society is likely to increase unless these issues are addressed. This disintegration our chickens coming home to roost after decades of destruction of our social capital'[sic]. (September 17)

'While the immediate objective may be bringing to justice the organisers of the dreadful hijackings on September 11, we must not stop there. We must take on with a new resolve the forces at the root of the attack. We must hunt them down and eradicate these scourges against freedom, democracy, justice for peace-loving people around the world: world debt, poverty and disenfranchisement of dispossessed peoples. Of course there will be some collateral damage. Global companies may need to pay sweat-shop workers a decent wage. Banks and other large investors may need to cancel loans. Overdeveloped countries may need to acknowledge that their wealth has come from centuries of colonial and post-colonial domination, exploitation and interference in internal political affairs of countries in the poorer parts of the world'. (September 19)

'Economically, we collectively hoard most of the world's wealth and this needs addressing. But when we also attempt, consciously or otherwise, to impose western culture, we start to create deep seated resentment among others. These others have included peoples of Muslim countries. Is our culture superior? I would argue we have lost touch with culture in the west. Is Nintendo, *Neighbours* and drugs culture? As we move more to the 'rational' we are moving further away from culture … Surely it is the west that should look at its own culture. This is what people of the east despise about the west, not our economics but the culture that goes with it. The culture of intolerance, crime, excess and materialism'. (October 19)